Real
HOPE in CHICAGO

The publication of this book commemorates Wayne L. Gordon's twenty years in ministry

Real
HOPE in CHICAGO

The incredible story of how the Gospel is transforming a Chicago neighborhood

Wayne L. Gordon
with *Randall Frame*

Foreword by John Perkins
with photos by William Favata

ZondervanPublishingHouse
Grand Rapids, Michigan

A Division of HarperCollins*Publishers*

Real Hope in Chicago
Copyright © 1995 by Wayne L. Gordon

Requests for information should be addressed to:

 ZondervanPublishingHouse
Grand Rapids, Michigan 49530

Library of Congress Cataloging-in-Publication Data

Gordon, Wayne.
 Real hope in Chicago : the incredible story of how the Gospel is saving a city /
Wayne L. Gordon with Randall Frame.
  p.   cm.
 ISBN 0-310-20553-0 (pbk.)
  1. Lawndale Community Church (Chicago, Ill.)—History.   2. Church work
with the poor—Illinois—Chicago.   3. Chicago (Ill.)—Church history—20th
century.   4. Gordon, Wayne.   5. Evangelicalism—Illinois—Chicago—History—
20th century.   I. Frame, Randall L.   II. Title.
 BX9999.C453667   1995
 289.9'5'0977311—dc20   95-31216
                                                                  CIP

Edited by Lyn Cryderman
Interior and cover photographs by William Favata

Printed in the United States of America

95 96 97 98 99 00 01 02 /❖ DH/ 10 9 8 7 6 5 4 3 2 1

To my wife, Anne,
and our three children,
Angela, Andrew, and Austin,
for teaching me, encouraging me, loving me,
and living out the Lawndale Miracle with me

CONTENTS

FOREWORD
by John Perkins

TALK WITH WAYNE GORDON for five minutes and you'll understand why anyone would want to call him friend. Ten minutes with him will help you understand why he is the type of Christian role model our cities desperately need. Spend fifteen years with him, laugh with him, struggle, dream, and cry with him, as I have, and you'll understand why I feel privileged and grateful to call him my friend and my brother in Christ.

Twenty years ago, Wayne was a recent college graduate with a degree and a burden to be the type of Christian he thought God wanted him to be. The all-American type kid from Iowa, an athlete-turned-coach, Wayne wanted to make a difference in the lives of young people in Chicago's inner city. He got a job and a vision, and both found him in a part of the Windy City most white Christians avoid.

To everyone's surprise, Wayne then moved into the Lawndale neighborhood where he was working, the only white person for miles, and started a Bible study with the young athletes he was coaching. And as if that weren't enough, he did what many thought was crazy: he stayed. For twenty years, he hung in there. He got married there. He raised his children there. He called Lawndale his home. Why? Partly because of his competitive nature, his enormous heart, and his inexhaustible drive, and partly because he never thought about failure, Wayne chose to live among, and identify with, the people he wanted to reach with the good news of Jesus Christ.

9

More amazing still is the fact that "Coach" (as he's known to his friends) still lives in Lawndale today. The young college graduate of twenty years ago simply wanted to serve God instead of serving himself. As a result, he now finds himself serving as the co-pastor of a 500-member multicultural church, overseeing numerous church-related holistic ministries that employ almost 150 people (many of whom are from the neighborhood), and working with me as president of our national network of urban ministries, the Christian Community Development Association (CCDA).

Lawndale Community Church and Wayne Gordon are really a testimony to the grace of God and the witness of God's call upon a person's life. After leaving college, Coach heard the missionary call of God and relocated to Lawndale, choosing an incarnational lifestyle where his neighbor's felt needs became his own. It was God's grace that sent him there, and God's grace that planted and grew Lawndale Community Church out of that first Bible study. By relocating to the community, he gained more opportunities to win people to Christ than he ever expected.

But it wasn't always easy, especially because he was a white man living in a black neighborhood. In Iowa and at Wheaton College, Coach hadn't learned much about the African-American culture. He did know, though, that the heart of the Gospel was reconciliation, and its power transcended any racial barriers. So he went to work in trying to reconcile people to God and to each other. That he actually moved into Lawndale to live among his black students reflects Wayne's deep commitment to and understanding for his mission as an ambassador of reconciliation.

This step toward racial reconciliation gave Coach still another opportunity to minister in a creative and essential way to his troubled community: empowering the youth. As he invested his own life and other resources into these young people, they responded in positive and powerful ways. Many have gone on to college; many have also come back to Lawndale, now as leaders and role models to youths who were once like they were. Because of Wayne's ability to redistribute resources and to empower people, he has probably done more than any other person I've known for raising up indigenous leaders, who in this case happen to be black.

It was no accident, then, that when the need arose for a CCDA president, I knew Wayne was just the right leader. I am often asked if whites can do effective ministry among African-Americans. Wayne Gordon is my answer. His personal life, community experiences and spiritual character exemplify the values I have taught for years in the work of Christian community development: relocation, reconciliation, and redistribution. Coach is a gifted and enthusiastic leader who is effective around anyone because he is not threatened by people. I believe that's part of where his stamina has come from, a stamina that has enabled him to stay in Lawndale for twenty years, surviving at least eleven break-ins in his home and numerous cross-cultural challenges, a stamina essential for leadership in a grass-roots movement such as CCDA.

I have great confidence in and appreciation for the friendship I have with Wayne, his wife, Anne, and their three children, and the ministry they share. That's why I believe this book is not only a timely model for Christian community development but an inspiration for those who would like to follow in his footsteps. This book offers an important challenge to other suburban folks: follow Wayne's example to cross economic and racial barriers and dare to enter the mission field of the inner city. Wayne and dozens of people are the better for it. And if others follow, then his work will have multiplied, and together, we as God's people will rebuild our urban communities for Christ.

I highly recommend this book for all people interested in the future of our cities and in Christian community development. Wayne Gordon's story and message are crucial reminders of the power of God's call if we'll only respond.

ACKNOWLEDGMENTS

THIS BOOK HAS BEEN made possible by the work of many people who God has used in the life of my family, the people of Lawndale, and me personally. There are too many whose names will never appear and will never be known except by God. Special thanks to the following:

All the fantastic people of Lawndale Community Church who have taught me so much and enriched my life with purpose and fulfillment on this earth.

The people of the CCDA movement across our nation where I have met thousands who have moved into impoverished areas and are living for Christ and his Kingdom. They inspire me every day.

The CCDA Board who have cried with me and have been supportive through many difficult times.

The Outreach Council of Lawndale Community Church: Carey Casey, Edward Daniels, Tami Doig, Pat Herrod, Andrew Moore, Tom Moore, and Stacey Smith, for walking and talking me through this task.

My mom, Deleina Gordon, who has always believed in me.

Guido Marchetti and his vision for having a spiritual impact on the athletes and students at Farragut High School.

Jim and Judy Caraher, Brink and Patricia Dickerson, Pat and Gretchen McMaskey, Glen and Carol Solheim of our Chicago Bible study, who have supported and encouraged Anne and me for years.

Art and Linda Jones, who were the first to relocate and join Anne and me on this journey.

Three people who are watching from heaven: Bill Leslie, my encourager; Tom Skinner, my empowerer; and Lyle Gordon, my earthly dad.

Precious Thomas, Willette Grant, Donna Holt, Carrie Moore, who inspire me every day.

Randy Frame, who has been able to capture my heart and put it into words. His help in writing has been extraordinary.

INTRODUCTION

I LOVE LIVING IN Lawndale.

I can't deny we have problems here. Often as I lie in my bed at night I hear gunshots outside on the street. When I moved here twenty years ago, the gunshots were usually separated by at least a second or two, but semiautomatic weapons have changed all that. These days, the bangs follow much more quickly, one after another. Modern technology has made killing another human being far more efficient.

Statistically, North Lawndale, on Chicago's West Side, is the country's fifteenth poorest neighborhood, and it also ranks that high in violence. In my twenty years in the city, I have seen death up close. I have preached at more funerals than I care to think about. Most of the victims were young men—boys really—some of whom I loved as a father loves a son.

I walk the streets alert but not alarmed. My wife and I are more concerned about our three children. We insist on knowing where they are every moment of every day. Our home and our church have been robbed—and our vehicles broken into or stolen—more times than we can recall.

In two decades of ministry here, I have witnessed the beguiling evil of drugs and the despair spawned by joblessness, homelessness, teen pregnancy, absentee parenthood, and other social pathologies. At times I have been angry, confused, discouraged, and afraid. But twenty years later I would not trade my time here—not one moment of it—for anything.

Writing this book has given me a chance to reflect. I have cried more in the few intense weeks of working on it than during the past several years combined. Some were tears of sadness for people I loved and now miss. But most were tears of joy as I recounted the overwhelming evidence of God's faithfulness, as I experienced again the contentment that results not from circumstances but from knowing and depending on God. I have witnessed amazing acts of sacrifice, commitment, and courage during my time here. I have felt the love and joy born out of a community of believers united in purpose, a community that claims life in the midst of death, victory in the midst of hopelessness.

The story of Lawndale Community Church is, at its heart, a story of how God is working—at times miraculously—in urban America through his community of persistent faith. Within that context, I am indebted to the people of Lawndale—especially my brothers and sisters in Christ—who enriched my life beyond measure as we walked together through moments of trial and times of celebration.

This is primarily *their* story, not mine. Each giant step we have taken has come at their initiative. In times when I doubted, others prayed in faith. At critical junctures when decisions had to be made, this community took risks and dreamed dreams too great for my imagination. Without their vision we would surely have perished long ago.

That is why I am uncomfortable when people portray me as a Christian hero, as sometimes happens. Had I entered urban ministry strictly out of some sense of obligation and self-sacrifice, perhaps I would deserve some earthly credit. But what sacrifice is there in doing something I have wanted to do and felt called to do since the days of my youth?

Throughout my life, I have had options and opportunities that my neighbors here in Lawndale have not had. The people here have experienced more personal tragedy and overcome greater odds than I have ever had to face. They are the true heroes, though if you ask the people of Lawndale, they would say there are no heroes but God. The testimonies you will encounter in the following pages can be understood only in the light of a faithful, loving, powerful, and personal God of miracles.

Together we, the people of Lawndale Community Church, have lived what we call the "Lawndale Miracle." Within this miracle, I believe, can be found the source of real hope for Chicago—indeed, for the world.

Part 1

Proclaim Good News to the Poor

One

JoJo: Release
the Oppressed

Dear Coach:

I have a very bad problem in my life right now. I
don't know if you can help me, but I really need help
right now. I know I been try to come back to church, but I
have not try hard enough. I had fun when I was in FCA
[Fellowship of Christian Athletes] and I'm sorry that I left.
I try to write this letter a month ago but I couldn't. But I'm
tired of life bein' like this. I'm very sorry Coach that I had
to tell you this. My problem is cocaine. It has really mess
up my life and I don't know what to do. Sometime I be
want to kill myself and maybe I will one day, but Coach,
I don't want to do that. But don't want to keep living my
life like this. Coach, you have done a lot for me in my life.
And I'm very sorry I let you down.

JOE ATKINS

It is unusual to take on a nickname later in life, but for as
long as I have been in Lawndale, people have called me
"Coach." To high school youth, senior citizens, neighbors,
policemen, and people on the church staff, I am still "Coach,"
even fourteen years after leaving a coaching position at
nearby Farragut High School.

I started at Farragut in 1975. I taught history and coached
football and wrestling until 1981. About six years later Joe's

letter was pushed under the door to my office at Lawndale Community Church, where I was pastor. In the upper left-hand corner of the envelope, where the return address is usually written, a single word was scrawled: *Scared.*

I can't remember a time when I did not know "JoJo" Atkins. I coached him at Farragut, where he wrestled in the lighter weight divisions. After my marriage in 1977 to Anne Starkey, JoJo would stop by our apartment almost every day. He had helped us move into it, paint it, and fix it up. He would hang out with us for ten or more hours a day. He and a friend declared themselves Anne's "bodyguards." JoJo had been nine years old when his father died. He became like a son to me.

Our place was a center of attraction for many Lawndale youth. We had installed a first-class weight machine and a Ping-Pong table in the storefront just below our apartment. When young men from the community came to exercise and play Ping-Pong, some of them would stay for Bible study or other ministry activities. JoJo attended the Bible studies faithfully. In 1978 he was even part of the founding of Lawndale Community Church: fifteen people attended our first worship service; JoJo was among them.

A year or so after graduating from high school, JoJo joined the Army, and I lost touch with him for a while. In the military, he experimented with drugs, and by the time he left, he was a veteran abuser, having tried them all: marijuana, heroin, and cocaine, to which he became addicted.

When JoJo returned to Lawndale, things weren't the same. He attended church sporadically. He would hang out on the streets, doing odd jobs to scrape a meager living. He did not look like his old self. I knew he was struggling, but I would never have guessed he was so heavily into cocaine.

JoJo

Then came the letter, an uninhibited cry for help. I met with JoJo and offered to do what I could for him. We talked about getting him into a drug rehabilitation program, but it soon became clear how strong a grip cocaine had on his life. I prayed for JoJo, but I felt helpless. He wanted to get straightened out, but—as I have learned many times during my time here—when drugs are involved, sometimes wanting something is not enough.

On April 21, 1987, six months or so after he wrote that letter, JoJo crawled into the bathtub in his apartment, cut his wrists open, and fell asleep. He awoke at 7:00 A.M. and was surprised to be alive. After wrapping something around his wrists, he walked to the church and entered my office to tell me what he had done. Immediately I called Art Jones, the doctor who founded our medical center, and he came over to sew up JoJo's wrists.

After seeing the blood in the bathroom at the apartment, where I had gone to collect his things, I quietly thanked God that JoJo was still with us. But God and I both knew it was just a matter of time before drugs would win this battle for JoJo's life—unless something changed. That same morning, JoJo agreed to enter the Teen Challenge drug rehabilitation program.

JoJo stayed in the program for three months before he left—too soon. Our church reached out to him, and he began to come around a little more often. But every time he seemed to be making progress, the lure of drugs would recapture him.

After several months of this tug-of-war, JoJo came to me again, pleading for help. I invited him to move into the church to sleep at night. I told him I would counsel him, meet with him, and pray with him every day, but he felt he needed more than that. And I am sure he was right. Having run into someone on the street who had successfully kicked drugs through a Christian drug rehabilitation program, JoJo decided to get into the same program, which consisted of nine months of inpatient treatment.

JoJo's victory in his personal war with drugs walked hand in hand with his deepening faith in Jesus Christ. Not only did he thrive at the drug treatment house but he became a leader there, counseling, encouraging, and praying with other young men.

JoJo called me frequently and stopped by sometimes to keep me posted on his progress. On one of these visits, I asked him, "JoJo, what's your dream?"

"Coach," he responded, "my dream is to have a house where I could work with men who are trying to get off of drugs."

Interestingly enough, our church had been dreaming about starting a home for men attempting to conquer drugs. Rarely a day goes by in Lawndale that I don't see someone selling drugs. The problem reached epidemic proportions long ago. Virtually every family in Lawndale has experienced firsthand the plague of drug abuse. But JoJo knew firsthand that there is a power greater than drugs.

At this writing, we are just a few months away from completing renovation of a building in which about twenty-five men will live as they attempt to overcome drug addiction and, hopefully, move on to become productive citizens in the kingdom of God. It will be called Hope House, and it will be managed by a young man I have known for a long time. His name is Joseph Atkins.

I still call him JoJo.

Two

Stanley: Freedom for the Prisoners

I MET STANLEY RATLIFF not long after moving to Lawndale. He played football at Farragut, during my time as defensive coordinator under coach Guido Marchetti. Stanley was a junior in high school when I met him, and we hit it off. Off the field we would get together, talk, go out for burgers, or just hang out.

Stanley was with me the night I faced my first physical assault in Lawndale. It was a pleasant, warm September evening, and we had decided to go over to Sixteenth Street after practice to get some ice cream. Sixteenth is known as one of the more dangerous streets in Chicago, and that night it lived up to its reputation.

Not long after we had entered the ice cream parlor, a man came in, pulled a knife on us, and said he wanted our money. I was scared. Though six years Stanley's senior, I looked to him for guidance on how to respond. I was still new in Lawndale and didn't know what to expect. Stanley kept his cool and encouraged this guy to do the same. With the situation about as tense as it could be, another man came in off the street. It didn't take long to conclude that this second fellow had had a little too much to drink. He started yelling at the guy with the knife, and before long they were

engaged in a big argument. Stanley and I seized the opportunity to slip out the door, hop into my old van, and get out
of there as fast as we could.

That incident was just one of many things that drew
Stanley and me together. Sometimes we ventured out into
the western suburbs to watch football games at Wheaton
College, my alma mater. Often he simply came over to my
apartment to visit.

At Farragut, Coach Marchetti and I started a Bible study
under the auspices of the Fellowship of Christian Athletes,
and we invited everyone on the team to come. Stanley attended every meeting, even though he never went to church.
In time Stanley made a commitment to Christ, though he had
a lot to learn about what that meant for his life.

During Stanley's senior year at Farragut, the football
team went undefeated, and Stanley had a great year as well,
both as a defensive end and a wide receiver. Through all his
success, he continued to come to Bible studies and to grow as
a young believer.

As with JoJo, when Stanley graduated from high school,
I began to lose touch with him. After entering college at
Northeastern Illinois University on Chicago's North Side,
Stanley did not come by very often. In those days, I was
lucky to see him once a year. In the mid-1980s he began delivering our mail, so I saw him a little more often then. By
then we had started the church, but he attended only a few
times a year.

In 1989, however, Stanley got into trouble. He had been
living with a woman named Antoinette, who had borne his
child, and they were having financial problems. One night an
acquaintance of theirs came to their apartment and offered to
help out. This man whipped out a wad of hundred-dollar
bills and laid ten of them on the kitchen table, telling Stanley

STANLEY

to pay him back when he got the chance. Stanley took the money, paid his bills, and was soon able to pay off the debt.

A few months later Stanley was riding in a car with this man, when the man asked Stanley to pull the car over. The man proceeded to give Stanley a small Walgreens Drugstore bag and asked him to deliver it to the woman sitting in a car up ahead.

Suspecting that drugs were in the bag, Stanley at first refused, but the man pointed out that Stanley owed him a favor. Grudgingly Stanley agreed to make the delivery. The woman asked him to sit in the car for a moment, and she tried to give Stanley money for the bag. Instead of taking the cash, however, Stanley tried to bolt from the car, but both he and the man who'd put him up to this job were immediately surrounded by police. The woman in the car pulled out a gun; she was an undercover Chicago police officer. Not surprisingly, the bag was full of cocaine.

Stanley got carted off to jail and was released on bond, pending a trial. The next day he came to my office to tell me about the trouble he was in. During this time of crisis, he started attending church regularly. He and Andrew Moore, who had played football with Stanley at Farragut, started meeting with me every Wednesday morning at six o'clock for Bible study. We met for an hour and a half each week to talk about our struggles and to pray. From time to time Stanley would report on his latest court appointment as the case against him dragged on. I had planned to testify as a character witness on his behalf.

One Wednesday, however, Stanley did not show up. Andrew and I both knew something was wrong. Stanley called to tell me he was in jail and that suddenly his case went to trial without my knowing. It lasted less than one day, and a jury convicted him of selling drugs.

Several people from the church attended Stanley's sentencing hearing, including Antoinette. The prosecution sought a twenty-five-year sentence, but the judge genuinely seemed to believe that Stanley had got a raw deal. He acknowledged that Stanley had never been arrested before, that he held a good job, and that he did not fit the stereotype of a felon. He explained, however, that his hands were tied, since, given the amount of cocaine in the bag, nine years was the minimum sentence that could be given in the State of Illinois.

I wept uncontrollably right there in the courtroom as they took Stanley away to prison. I knew beyond doubt—and I think the judge knew it too—that Stanley was a victim of circumstances. But such is life for black youth in the city, even those not inclined toward crime.

Every Friday, Stanley called me collect from prison. We talked and prayed together. Every few months I made the hundred-mile trip to visit him in Dixon, Illinois. Sometimes people from the church went with me.

It was clear that Antoinette was struggling. She now had two small children to take care of, and she could not always pay the rent. So the church adopted her and her two boys, Antwane and Antonio, and moved them into one of the apartments we owned.

As the appeals process dragged on Antoinette began to lead the charge for Stanley's release. She wrote the governor, explaining the case and asking for a pardon. She got me and others to write letters on Stanley's behalf. I complied, even though I figured this effort had no chance of succeeding. But lo and behold, in 1991 Stanley was granted a hearing before the governor's prisoner review board, which makes recommendations on clemency. Four of us from the church went to testify, and I delivered what I think was the most moving and persuasive sermon I have ever preached.

In most cases that come before the review board, the pattern was familiar: a defense attorney argues on behalf of the defendant, while the prosecutor claims the convicted criminal is a menace to society. In contrast, we did not even have a defense attorney. As for the prosecutor from the state's attorney's office, he told the review board that he would be happy to answer questions, but he never suggested that Stanley should remain in prison. A few minutes later the prosecutor pulled me aside and confided that he did not believe Stanley should have been put in prison in the first place. Amazingly, he said he planned to stay until all the other cases had been heard so he could let some of the members of the review board know that he thought Stanley was innocent.

This took place in December 1991. Although things did not move as quickly as we would have liked, on a Friday morning in February 1992, I got a call from Antoinette. She said she had just talked with Stanley's mother. The governor's office had just called her with the news that Stanley had received a pardon. Antoinette asked me if I could go to Dixon to get him, and before long I was on my way.

My son, Austin, who was three at the time, accompanied me to the prison. On our way back home, Stanley and I spent most of the time shouting, singing, and praising God. As we arrived at Stanley's home we saw a crowd of people had gathered, including Stanley's mother and a couple of his siblings. Antoinette stood there, holding Stanley's baby son, whom he had never seen. As we pulled up ten-year-old Antonio ran to his dad. He leaped into Stanley's arms, and Stanley dropped his bags and threw his arms around him as the boy cried over and over, "Daddy, I love you."

Our Sunday service that weekend focused on one thing: celebration. We sang and danced and jumped up and down. Most of all, we praised God for his faithfulness.

I asked Stanley about what it was like in prison. "You know, Coach," he said, "it wasn't that bad." While in prison Stanley had completed his college degree. He had led the music every week at Bible study and for the Sunday morning worship. He had read through the Bible at least twice and had regularly shared his faith with others. As with JoJo, God had used crisis to draw Stanley nearer.

During the time Stanley was in prison, we talked frequently about a prison wedding for him and Antoinette, for despite their strong commitment to one another, the two had never exchanged vows. Two weeks after he was released, we had the wedding during Sunday morning worship. We typically do this in cases in which people have been living together, for it gives them a way of acknowledging that this aspect of their lives was not pleasing to God but that they now desire to live together in Christ.

The church was unusually crowded and bustling with excitement that morning. The only problem was that when it came time for the ceremony, Antoinette was nowhere to be found. She was still at home, taking as much time as possible in making sure everything was just exactly right. I finally had to leave the church to go get her. For the people, however, the morning was worth the wait. The wedding and the reception that followed resumed the celebration that had begun a few weeks earlier.

Today there is a tremendous man of God at Lawndale Community Church who serves the church full-time as an assistant pastor in charge of our worship and music. He also has an outreach ministry to men in prison, and he works with JoJo at Hope House, ministering to men recently released from prison. His name is Stanley Ratliff.

TOP CAT

A high school teacher's dream is not to have all straight-A students but to succeed at turning a wayward student's life around, to get him or her excited about learning, to provide a sense of purpose in life. At least, that was my goal at Farragut High School. Every day, I tried to call each of my students by name or give them a pat on the back or say something to let them know I cared.

One of the students in my U.S. history class in 1976 went by the nickname Top Cat. At eighteen years of age, he should have already graduated, but he hardly ever showed up for class. One day I stopped him outside and told him I thought he could do a good job in my class. I challenged him to come and give it a try.

The next day he took me up on the challenge and came to class. I soon realized that what Top Cat wanted was what all young people desire and need: a little personal attention. He started coming to my class every day and went from failing to becoming a straight-A student.

One morning, however, Top Cat did not show up. It was the first class he had missed in months. I asked the other students if they knew anything. One of them spoke up: "You ain't heard, Coach? Top Cat got shot last night over on Sixteenth Street. He was in on that robbery at the gas station. He got shot in the back. He's dead."

My eyes filled with tears. I could not gather myself to teach my class. I had the class read from their textbooks instead. Part of what bothered me was the students' indifference to the news. One of their classmates had died tragically, and they gave me the news as if it were a weather report. Their young lives had already been numbed to violence and death.

Wanting to attend Top Cat's funeral, I tried desperately to get some information. Top Cat had no phone. I had no way to get in touch with his family. I didn't even know if he had a family. I watched all the TV news shows, but could find nothing about Top Cat's funeral or the robbery. I scanned the *Chicago Tribune* and again came up empty. The same with the *Sun-Times*. I read the *Chicago Defender*, a newspaper that targets Chicago's African-American community, cover to cover and found not a word about my prize student and my friend, Top Cat.

So I never got to grieve at his funeral. I don't know if he even had one. A passage in Psalm 72 states, "Precious is the blood of people." I realized in 1976 that this was true only for some in our society. It certainly did not seem to apply to Top Cat. He died anonymously. No one cared. No one's life missed a beat. He was a "nobody," a discarded person—exactly the kind of person Jesus came to save.

X   X   X

Three

Donna and Robert: Proclaim the Year of the Lord's Favor

NOT EVERY SUCCESS STORY at Lawndale Community Church results from a life crisis.

For as long as I have known Robert Holt, he has lived an upright, model Christian life, even though by most standards the odds were stacked against him, since he grew up in the "projects" without a father around. Robert stood out, both as a football player and a wrestler at Farragut. He attended Bible study faithfully and has been a part of the church almost from its beginning.

I'll never forget the day Robert jogged off the field during a football game to tell me his arm hurt. Since his arm looked fine to me, I gave him a pat on the back and sent him back into the game. The next day he showed up in church with a cast on his arm—ruining my chances of ever getting into med school. Robert had played almost half a game with a broken arm! Naturally, I felt terrible, but in all the years I've known him, he has never held it against me.

On another occasion, I was waiting in the gymnasium for my wrestling team to come up from the basement locker rooms. Our opponents were ready to go. The referee came over to me and said we would have to forfeit the first match if my team did not show up soon.

Furious, I went down the stairs to the locker room, ready to give those kids a tongue-lashing for messing around so long. But as soon as I entered the locker room, I saw what was holding them up. My team had gathered in the middle of the room, and they were on their knees with their hands together—praying. Robert and another young man named Carl Hill were the ringleaders. I listened as they quietly prayed—not for victory but for the strength to be witnesses for Christ. Who says there is no prayer in public schools! I marched back upstairs and told the ref my guys were in the middle of something very important and would arrive soon enough.

Nothing has ever stood in the way of Robert's commitment to Christ. After high school he went to Olivet Nazarene College. To pay his way, he worked from midnight to 4:00 A.M. almost every night for UPS, washing trucks and wrapping packages. It took him five years to graduate from Olivet, but he stayed the course. Upon his graduation UPS offered him a full-time job as a supervisor, and before long he was on a career track, headed for a management position. Yet through all this success, he never strayed from his faith. He stayed true to the Lord all the way.

During his college years, Robert attended the church as often as he could. There he had the chance to stay in touch with a young woman named Donna Lynn, who had begun attending Bible studies at the church as an eighth-grader. When Donna arrived at Farragut as a freshman, Robert, a senior, looked out for her in a sort of big-brother role. Eventually their relationship turned into something more. They stayed in touch after Robert went off to college.

DONNA AND ROBERT

As a sophomore in high school, Donna began working at the church for a couple of hours a day as my secretary. I'll never forget the time she came into my office after typing something I'd dictated. She said, "Coach, I think you made a mistake here."

I said, "What do you mean?"

"Well," she answered, "you wrote here that Lawndale's a poor community and that the people of Lawndale are poor. Coach, I'm not poor. And Lawndale is not a poor neighborhood."

I pointed out to Donna that she had been reared by a mother on welfare.

She responded, "Being on welfare doesn't make you poor."

As I continued to talk with Donna that afternoon a new definition of poverty began to emerge in my mind. I realized that poverty has nothing to do with how much money a person makes. Rather it is a state of mind. Donna did not allow herself to be considered poor. From that day on I became much more careful about calling people poor. For one thing, labeling someone "poor" has a way of making them live that way.

Donna soon became like a daughter to Anne and me, joining us for dinner and baby-sitting for our children. She attended a Christian college. I remember the day I drove her there and sent her off with a big hug.

I also remember her pain in the months that followed as she experienced—for the first time in her life—racism, as people said and assumed certain things about her based strictly on the color of her skin. To be sure, some charges of racism are open to interpretation, but I had no doubt that what Donna had experienced was real. So she transferred to another school after a year and had a much better experience there.

During her senior year in college, I had the privilege of marrying Donna and Robert at our church. The temperature was ninety-five degrees, and there was no air-conditioning, but that did not detract from the joy I felt as she walked down that aisle to where Robert and I waited for her.

Few things are more rewarding in pastoral ministry than to see two people who have followed Christ from their earliest days come together in holy matrimony. Here was a young man I had helped lead to Christ and later baptized in Lake Michigan, a man who, like the woman he was marrying, had followed the Lord for all of his days. It was especially rewarding in this community—where sex before marriage is almost a given—to celebrate the union of a couple who resisted the temptation and did it God's way.

If Lawndale's present reality revolves primarily around meeting people in crisis, Donna and Robert epitomize our future. Their children will grow up with both a father and a mother, immersed in values that stand against the values of the world.

Robert stayed with UPS and in 1990 was transferred to St. Louis. While many people grow up with the dream of leaving Lawndale, Donna and Robert's dream was to return. After living in St. Louis for three years, they began to pray for opportunities to get back home. Their prayers were answered when Robert applied for an opening at the UPS office in Rockford, Illinois, and was accepted. Donna took a job in the corporate world and quickly began moving up her own career ladder.

But money and prestige are no match for the joy of being involved in an active ministry that changes lives. Today the Holts are back in Lawndale. Robert commutes to Rockford, while Donna serves as the director of the Christian Community Development Association's national headquarters, located here in Lawndale. She is also active in various ministries of the church, such as leading women's aerobics and directing our choir. As I write this book Donna and Robert are expecting their first child.

PART 2

The Lawndale Miracle

Four

The Right Side
of the Tracks

IN FORT DODGE, IOWA, I had the great privilege of growing up
on the wrong side of the tracks. That is to say, I grew up on
the same side of the tracks as the African Americans in my
town. As far as I was concerned, of course, ours was the right
side of the tracks. I believe that while I was in my mother's
womb God created a special place in my heart for the vul-
nerable and oppressed people of the world, especially for
people of color.

I remember one of my teachers slapping a Cuban boy because he could not speak English very well. I made a point of
befriending him after that, even though it got me into trouble with some of my peers. This same teacher mistreated a
girl in my class, and it was obvious to me that the only reason was that Lenora Culps was black. I became Lenora's
friend too, unfazed by those who teased me by saying that
she was my girlfriend. I remember getting into fights defending African-American children when I felt they were
being mistreated.

Although I had attended church all my life, I did not totally surrender my life to Christ until the summer of 1969, at
the age of fifteen. I attended a Fellowship of Christian Athletes
camp at which a black man by the name of John Westbrook
spoke. John had broken the color barrier at Baylor University,

and he was also the first African American to play football in the Southwest Conference.

As he talked about the differences between going to church and being a Christian I began to realize that God wanted more from me. As John sang "I Believe," I cried and asked God to come into my life and take over. I spoke with John afterward and told him what I had done. He signed my Bible, writing in it the verse Galatians 2:20. Ever since then it has been my life verse: "I have been crucified with Christ and I no longer live, but Christ lives in me. The life I live in the body, I live by faith in the Son of God, who loved me and gave himself for me."

The following January as I prayed in bed one night I once again expressed my desire for God to use me. "I will do anything you want me to do," I prayed. I did not have a vision or hear an audible voice, but he spoke to my mind and my heart, giving me the clear message that I was to work with black people. My first thought was that I was being called to the mission field in Africa, but I quickly understood that my calling would be right here in America.

So powerful was this calling that I wanted to quit high school and get started the very next day. I got my mother out of bed at one in the morning. She explained to me that I would not be allowed to quit school, but she took my sense of calling very seriously. We prayed about it right then, and the next day she contacted our pastor, Dr. Vernon Pearson.

While some people—even pastors—might have dismissed this whole thing as misguided youthful exuberance, Dr. Pearson pulled a book off the shelf and gave it to me to read: *Black and Free* by a young evangelist named Tom Skinner. Then, on my behalf, Dr. Pearson proceeded to contact Tom Skinner, David Wilkerson, and others who were

SUMMER DAY

active in urban ministry. They told him that once I finished high school, they would very much like to meet me.

Not wanting to wait that long, I decided to write to John Westbrook to tell him about my calling. He wrote back, informing me about a ministry to athletes in the inner city of Chicago. He gave me the names of Jim Queen and Ray Bakke. I called Jim Queen, and he invited me to join him in Chicago over the summer to work with youth, to play and coach baseball and basketball. He said he couldn't pay me much: ten dollars a week plus room and board.

As things turned out, I didn't even get room and board, since the ministry ran out of money. I lived with another young man who had come to spend his summer in the city. We lived on next to nothing in a condemned apartment building, yet I had a tremendously fulfilling experience—on and off the basketball court—as I ministered to these young men, some of whom were gang lords. I played on the Cabrini Green Housing Project's basketball team—the lone white guy.

Two experiences that summer confirmed that I was following the path God wanted me to follow. The first was when my apartment mate and I ran out of food and money. Up to that point, I had never gone a day in my life without eating. But on this occasion, I spent not one but three days on this unintentional fast. I don't recall how, but on the fourth day I was somehow able to scrounge up eighteen cents, just enough to buy a loaf of day-old bread. I consumed the entire loaf at one sitting. The next morning, the Scripture passage for my personal devotions happened to be Matthew 6, the passage that instructs us not to worry about what we will eat or drink or wear: "Seek ye first the kingdom of God, and his righteousness; and all these things shall be added unto you" (KJV).

There in the heart of America's "Second City," I got down on my knees by the side of my bed and confessed,

"God, I can't even feed myself. I'll depend on you to feed me."

That same day I opened my mail to find that the Beisser family from my home church had sent me twenty-five dollars. Two weeks later my pastor sent me another twenty-five dollars, which I again used for food. Then someone gave Jim Queen a hundred pounds of pancake batter! We had pancakes almost every day for the rest of the summer. I must confess that to this day I do not like pancakes. But back then they were manna in the desert. They served to build my faith that God would always provide.

Through the second experience I learned to trust that God would also protect. One night I found myself sharing my faith with a man who was about twenty years my senior. He invited me to his apartment to continue our conversation. Before long, however, I realized he was not interested in getting to know Christ. What he really wanted was to have sex with me. He expressed this desire while showing me some pornographic pictures. When I told him it was time for me to leave, he blocked my path to the door and hastily locked the chain.

Terrified, I prayed silently, imploring God to deliver me. I felt ill-equipped to protect myself, as this man was not only older but bigger. After I had refused his advances, he attempted to manipulate me psychologically by offering compromises, giving me choices about what I could do. Needless to say, I did not like any of the options. After about thirty minutes, he began to get more pushy, and I grew more scared.

Finally a plan came to my mind. As a ploy, I pretended to agree to one of his compromises. Thinking that I would follow through, he let his guard down. Waiting for the right moment, I ran at this guy as hard as I could. Using the best of my football skills, I tackled him, and as we wrestled there by the door I was able to disengage the chain. Whether God gave me supernatural strength or an extra dose of adrenaline, I don't know. But somehow I was able to throw this guy far enough across the room for me to get out the door. As I ran down the hallway I looked back over my shoulder and saw him reaching into his pocket. I feared he might have a gun or a knife, but I kept on running down the hallway, out of the apartment, and away from the building.

It never occurred to me to allow such a terrifying experience to dissuade me from my calling. What I learned from this—and from other experiences the summer of my sixteenth year—was that I could trust God in all situations. I returned to finish high school even more convinced of what the Lord wanted me to do.

After graduating, I enrolled at Wheaton College in the western suburbs of Chicago. I continued my athletic career on the gridiron. God continued to prepare me, through my Wheaton years, for ministry in the city. I elected courses and read books with that focus in mind. I went through a time when, despite the color of my skin, I tried to be black. God showed me, however, that I could never be black but that that did not matter. He was calling me, a white man, to minister in the black community, just as he called Paul, a Jew, to reach out to the Gentiles. Through the years, I have realized more than a few times what an unlikely candidate I was for urban ministry: a small-town boy from Iowa, I'm not a big man nor a rough-looking guy. Even in my forties, I am accused of having a baby face. It's just part of the Lawndale Miracle that God used an ordinary Christian like me to accomplish his purposes. All I ever did was to invite God to use me however he wanted.

Although Wheaton College is in the suburbs, my heart was always in the city. I typically traveled to Chicago three times a week to help out in various ministry projects. During this time, I began to realize just how shallow and meaningless a profession of faith in Christ can be—after all, some of the men on skid row whom I worked with would recommit their lives to Christ week after week yet still go on living in self-destructive ways. I began to understand that for evangelism to make any difference, it has to take place in the context of caring relationships.

After graduating from college, I began looking for an urban community in which I could work and live. I had determined while at Wheaton that my best entrée might be as a high school teacher and coach. Through the Fellowship of Christian Athletes, I heard about a man, Guido Marchetti, who had been head football coach at Farragut High School for sixteen years. Guido had just recently become a Christian. He was trying to get a Bible study started with his football team, but he didn't know how to go about it.

I stopped by to visit him, and together we went to the principal's office, where I was informed that no teaching jobs nor paid coaching positions were available. The best they could offer was to allow me to coach as a volunteer and to teach as a substitute, with no benefits, on an "as needed" basis. I accepted the offer, and as things turned out, I never missed a day.

I had been offered other jobs, including one back in my hometown in Iowa to work in the local school district as its liaison to the black community. It seemed perfect: good pay and benefits, the chance to return home, meaningful work that was consistent with my calling. But I was convinced the Lord had called me to the city. I'll never forget what the man who offered me the job in Iowa said to me when I turned it down. Despite telling me he respected me, he called me a "damn fool." Maybe so. But I'd rather be a "damn fool" at the center of God's will than a genius any-where else.

Eventually my teaching position at Farragut became a paid, full-time position, which I considered to be something of a miracle in itself, for before graduating from college, I had gone to the Chicago Board of Education with résumé in hand and with hopes of getting a position teaching history. The man there laughed at me and said they wouldn't have any openings in history for ten years. However, Arlene Daggs, the assistant principal at Farragut (she is still in that position today), had other ideas. I don't know exactly how she did it, but through some combination of playing with numbers and hiding me from the board for a while, she was able to create an opening.

I had the honor of personally delivering my letter of hire, written by Arlene, to the same man at the board of education who had laughed at me several months earlier. As I sat across his desk I asked, "Do you remember me?" When he said he did, I told him I got the position because God wanted me to be at Farragut. He said that must be true since he would have never dreamed an opening could be created so soon.

I loved my job at Farragut and the ministry opportuni-ties that came with it. After realizing that our football and wrestling teams were not as physically strong as those of other high schools, I decided we needed a good weight ma-chine. I sold my Model-A Ford, which had been sitting in my parents' garage in Iowa, for $1,500. A guy I knew in high school, Kim Beisser, sent another $500. The rest of the $3,000 we needed came in small spurts, but eventually we had enough. Almost every athlete and coach at Farragut helped paint and renovate the empty storefront in front of my apart-ment for the weight machine (since there was no room for it at the school). Before long we had Bible studies going, and young men were turning to the Lord.

I got a chance to meet literally thousands of young people, and I got to know as many of them personally as I could. Farragut was everything I'd imagined and hoped it would be. Several teachers supported me with advice and encouragement, including Mr. Marchetti and fellow coaches Wardell Vaughn and Jim Thompson, who are still friends of mine today. These men were able to discern the sincerity that lay beneath my naïveté. They were my teachers as I continued my efforts to understand African-American culture.

Everyone told me I was crazy for moving to Lawndale, which was and still is almost exclusively African American. They said the people would not allow me to live there. Christian people advised me not to move there, as did non-Christian people. Black people said it, as well as white folks. The teachers at Farragut said it too. But in my heart I knew I was supposed to live there. In moving to North Lawndale, I became the only teacher at Farragut—of any race or hue—to reside in the community. And before long it began to feel like home.

For me to live in Lawndale was one thing. But to bring my wife to live there was another. I met Anne Starkey, a native of Indianapolis, in 1976 at the funeral of a mutual friend. For me it was the proverbial love at first sight. It took her a bit longer, but eventually we realized things could get serious very quickly. Before our relationship got too far along, however, I informed Anne about my strong sense of calling to the city. I told her I had no plans to leave North Lawndale. Anne told me that she had never felt a similar call to ministry in the city but that, as Ruth followed Naomi, she would be willing to follow me and share my dream.

We got married in June 1977. Understandably, Anne's parents were apprehensive about their daughter moving into the city—and their first visit to Lawndale did nothing to put them at ease. The day after returning from our honeymoon, Anne and I picked them up—as well as her siblings, Jeff, Doug, and Susie—at the airport. After church and brunch, we returned to our apartment to find that someone had broken in and stolen two TVs, a stereo, and various other items. Charles and Ardelle Starkey's fears were instantly confirmed.

To make matters worse, the day was hot and sticky, and we had no air-conditioning. Most of the windows did not work. It was enough to make Anne's father physically sick. They had planned to stay with us for a few days but decided to head back to Indianapolis the next day.

That night, after her parents had gone to bed, I got down on my knees as Anne sat in a chair next to me. I said, "Honey, everyone advised me not to bring a wife into this neighborhood, particularly a white woman. Maybe what happened today was a sign from God. Maybe I made a mistake. Maybe I wasn't supposed to bring you to live in this community."

Without pausing, Anne looked directly into my eyes and said, "Honey, I love you and I want to live here."

As tears filled our eyes we held one another. We knew from that very first night that our journey might be a rough one, that it might be hard at times. But we also were confident that God had called us to do exactly what we were doing. That confidence has been reaffirmed time and again throughout our eighteen years together here.

Our apartment was broken into no fewer than ten times during our first three years of marriage. Each time was difficult. Once, we had left town for just half a day to meet Anne's parents, only to return and find the door broken in. We went through more TV sets than I can count. We would never replace them, however. Someone would always give us another one—only to have it disappear in the next break-in.

On one occasion, in the middle of the night, we were in the apartment when we heard someone breaking through the door downstairs. We called the police, but they did not respond right away. I do not own a gun, but by coincidence, a few days earlier I had brought one from Iowa so I could go hunting with one of my football players and his dad. I surprised myself by taking that gun and jumping out into the hallway when I heard footsteps coming up the stairs. Though the gun was not loaded, our unwelcome guest had no way of knowing that. After one look at me, he turned and ran outside as quickly as he could. As he made his escape my wife yelled at him through the upstairs window. When it was all over, the police finally arrived and helped us secure the door.

On Labor Day weekend of 1978, we went to Chicago's downtown area for the day and came back to an apartment virtually emptied of everything that would have any value for a thief—including our typewriter, a calculator, Anne's sewing machine, a couple of radios, and, yes, our television. We were devastated.

The next morning, a Sunday, I rose early to go to my church office, which at that time was right below our apartment. That too had been robbed. I lost all my power tools, another typewriter, and various other items. I put my face in my hands and cried.

After composing myself, I called one of my former professors at Wheaton College, Don Church, known affectionately to me and many others as "Bubba." I said to him, "Bubba, I don't know if I can go on. We've been broken into again." I told him I didn't know if I could even muster the energy to go up and tell Anne what had happened. Telling Anne was always the hardest part.

Bubba prayed with me over the phone. He talked with me and encouraged me to try to see the bigger picture. I changed my sermon topic that morning and decided to preach out of 2 Corinthians 11, which addresses the hardships encountered by the apostle Paul, including being shipwrecked and beaten. I confessed that I felt beaten down, unsure if I could continue. At one point I cried during the sermon, and so did Don Church, who was among the thirty or so people in attendance. Bubba and his wife, Ann, treated Anne and me to lunch that day. They prayed with us, and then Bubba helped me board up the broken holes the burglars had used as entrances.

At that time, Anne's father made a living by installing alarms in banks. So we decided to call him. He dropped everything and came to Chicago to help us. Unbelievably, even as we were installing the alarm in our apartment, I heard a noise in an adjoining unit where Jerry and Nancy Foster, a couple from the church, were living. Since I knew they were not home, I went over to check and discovered that a light I had purposely left on had been turned off. I called the police. When they arrived, Anne walked off one way with an officer, and I went up the back stairs with another. We discovered two guys—with a TV, stereo, and other items rolled up in a bedspread. They kept running even after the officer told them to stop, so I ran after them. Though they dropped the merchandise, we were not able to catch them. My father-in-law installed an alarm in that apartment too.

Eventually we moved into another apartment a block away (where we still live today) and had break-ins there as well. I remember with sadness the night I lost my high school class ring. Again my father-in-law came out to install another alarm. As we were working we heard a woman scream. Even though I had been married to Anne for about three years by then, I did not recognize it as her scream. But her father did. We ran out to the street to find Anne and Linda Jones, a newcomer to the community, running toward us. They had been jumped, and someone had tried to rip a gold chain from Linda's neck.

As of this writing, no one, to my knowledge, has attempted to break into our home for over ten years—though the last break-in was perhaps the most memorable. Anne and I were in Indianapolis visiting her parents. I was outside having personal devotions early one morning when Art Jones called us from Lawndale. I instinctively knew it must be bad news. Sure enough, he informed us that someone had broken into our apartment and stolen everything—in spite of the alarm system. Once more I faced the task of having to tell Anne. She was hurt and angry.

I was angry too—at God. I stormed outside and prayed, "God, why do you let this stuff happen? I've given up my life to follow you, to minister in the inner city. Why can't you at least protect my house?"

I never saw any redeeming purpose behind all the break-ins until a few years later when I was sitting alone one morning, reading Scripture and meditating. I began to perceive that God was trying to tell me something. He spoke to my heart about my attitude. He seemed to be saying, "You know all those break-ins you had? Well, you know, you came to this neighborhood thinking you were pretty good. But you know what? You've got an attitude problem. You think you're more important than other people. You think I love you more than the prostitute who lives next door or the drug addict down the street. But I love everybody the same. And you need to know that you can't demand preferential treatment. When it rains in Lawndale, it's going to rain on you too."

That morning, I repented of having a superior attitude. I began to distinguish between trusting in God's protection and demanding it. I began to reject thoughts that God was going to treat me better because I was doing him a favor. I realized that God can accomplish anything he wants to in Lawndale, with or without me. In fact, God was the one doing me a favor by allowing me the privilege of living among and learning from the people of North Lawndale, of being a part of a ministry that has provided more fulfillment than I could have ever imagined.

Five

Learning to Listen

WHEN I MOVED to North Lawndale in 1975, it was one of Chicago's toughest neighborhoods. But things were not always that way. Many people from the community—and from our church—remember better days when Lawndale was inhabited by hardworking, community-minded citizens. It had been originally settled by middle-class people of Jewish and Bohemian descent. African Americans began arriving in the 1950s, and until the mid-1960s this was a safe place to live and work—businesses thrived, and people were proud to live here, proud to call it their home.

All that changed during the decade of the 1960s. As happened throughout America, people began to follow the lure of the suburbs, seeking better employment opportunities, lower cost of living, and cheaper real estate, financed and encouraged by the Federal Housing Administration (FHA). As racial tensions heightened, white folks began to leave Lawndale out of fear or because real estate agents had convinced them that the presence of blacks would devalue their homes. The more unscrupulous of these agents exploited both white and black people, persuading whites to sell low out of desperation and then turning around to sell high to the blacks moving in.

Gradually businesses began to leave; International Harvester, Sears, and Western Electric were among the major companies that left Lawndale. It is estimated that our community lost 120,000 jobs between 1960 and 1970. Denominational churches participated in the migration; only the Roman Catholic Church remained in any significant way.

But Lawndale's fate was sealed when many of its present and future community leaders—including educated African Americans—found their way to the suburbs or to other parts of Chicago. The net effect was to leave a vacuum at the heart of this inner-city community.

Vacuums, however, do not remain empty for long. Drug dealers filled the vacuum created by the loss of legitimate business. Unable to find work, many young men turned to crime. Those who maintained the values of the previous decades began to feel trapped. For many, the goal became to get out of Lawndale and never look back.

These conditions combined to give birth to today's Lawndale, which was featured in the 1986 book *The American Millstone* as representing urban America in rapid decline. This book deemed Lawndale to be part of this country's "permanent underclass." Based on external indicators, that assessment is hard to dispute. The break-ins, robberies, and vandalism described in the previous chapter are mere nuisances compared with the more serious crime that has become commonplace here. One act of violence takes place every three hours in our community of sixty-five thousand. Someone is shot almost every day. About sixty are murdered each year, while many others are permanently maimed or disabled as a result of violence.

Estimates place Lawndale as the nation's fifteenth poorest neighborhood. A person cannot buy a pair of shoes in Lawndale; there is no store that sells them. We have no chain grocery stores here, and we got our first and only McDonalds just three years ago. About seventy-five percent of our working-age people, according to most estimates, are

LANCE

unemployed. The median income of our community is below the national poverty rate, which means more than half earn less than fifteen thousand dollars a year.

More than fifty percent of Lawndale's residents receive some form of public assistance, and the current welfare system, as has been widely documented, serves only to make matters worse. (Let me say for the record, however, that in my view neither the Democrats nor the Republicans have a workable solution to the welfare problem.) The system rewards those who have babies outside of marriage. And those who genuinely want to get off welfare find it virtually impossible to do so, because they cannot survive on minimum wage, and their reward for getting a job is to have their government-assisted medical benefits taken away.

As for other social pathologies, nearly eighty percent of our children are born to unwed mothers, and most of those children have been abandoned by their fathers. Many of these mothers and children find it a challenge just to find a decent place to live. The seventy-seven communities defined by the city of Chicago are home to some seven thousand vacant lots. About a thousand of those are located in North Lawndale. The many abandoned, rat-infested buildings that were long ago boarded up have led some to observe that parts of our community resemble a war zone.

The average ACT score at Lawndale's two public high schools is slightly more than half the national average. Fewer than forty percent of the adults in our community graduated from high school, and only about forty percent of those who enter high school today will graduate. Even many of those who make it through high school will not have learned the skills they need to compete in the marketplace. Some are functionally illiterate. It is no wonder that during the Reagan years, Secretary of Education William Bennett came to this city at least half a dozen times and declared the Chicago public school system the worst in the nation.

But the biggest problem facing our community—by far—is hopelessness, which often leads to drugs. Drugs account for an overwhelming percentage of the violent crime in North Lawndale, and the problem has grown worse over the years. When I moved to the community, I would occasionally see someone smoking marijuana, or I might hear about someone dealing drugs. Today, within a five-block radius of our church, I can find at least seven or eight corners where drugs are exchanged almost every day. The price has come down to meet the market demand, with "crack" being the best-known case in point. Drug abuse renders its victims incapable of holding or pursuing a job or of caring for a family. And drug trafficking ties in heavily to illicit gang activity.

With such a dismal picture of conditions in North Lawndale, one might fairly wonder if there is any hope. My answer is a resounding "Yes!" This community's greatest asset has always been—and continues to be—its people. They are wonderful. Those of us who care about our community—and who know the difference between right and wrong—are blessed with an incredibly resilient and determined spirit. As this spirit grows and finds its hope in Jesus Christ amazing things can happen—as you will discover.

I experienced this positive community spirit from my earliest days here. When I moved into my first apartment on Fifteenth Street, I was the only white person on the block. It was one of the city's roughest streets, located just around the corner from a little liquor store known as the "Bucket of Blood" because of all the people who had been shot or stabbed there. Some of the kids from Farragut High School were afraid to come to my apartment for Bible study. It was the kind of place where you would expect people to look out only for themselves.

One day, however, upon returning from a trip to Iowa for Christmas, I discovered that someone had broken into my van. I was confused, though, to find the spare tire lying on the front seat. It looked as if someone had tried to steal it but had left it behind. I called the police. When they arrived, they informed me that three people on the street had called them when they witnessed a known heroin addict, who lived two doors down from me, trying to strip my van. After the police had caught the guy, my neighbors set up a community watch to make sure my tire wasn't stolen before I got back.

The point is this: these people sensed that I was a person of character, and therefore they were willing to report to the police someone they had known from childhood—simply because he was doing something wrong. These people were living out the dream of Martin Luther King Jr.—that people would be judged not by the color of their skin but by the content of their character.

I have experienced enough displays of moral integrity and selfless sacrifice over the years to become convinced that the answers to the problems of any community can be found right there in the neighborhood. I am further convinced that the keys to unlocking these answers can be summarized by a single word: *listening.* God gave us two ears and only one mouth for a reason!

Every significant step in bringing more hope and healing to this community has resulted from listening. It was out of listening to the community that Lawndale Community Church was born. I had been leading a Bible study for male athletes in the weight room below our apartment while Anne was leading a Bible study upstairs for teenage girls, and we heard one message over and over: many of those with whom we met enjoyed Bible study but did not like going to church. In January 1978, therefore, we challenged these young people to examine closely what the Bible says about church, and we concluded as a group that church is not about doctrines or denominations or nice buildings. It's about people committed to Jesus Christ who gather together to praise God.

Then one night the athletes in my Bible study asked me, "Coach, if that's what church is about, why can't we just start our own church, and you can be our pastor?"

I responded, "Well, I'll have to pray about that one," which of course is the card-carrying evangelical's way of saying, "No way." Anne and I had many ministry-related reasons for living in the city, but starting a church was not among them.

Later that night I told Anne, half smiling, about what my kids had proposed. Much to my surprise, she informed me that the girls in her study—along with Geraldine Moore, the mother of two of the boys—had suggested exactly the same thing. These young people were serious! We knew we had a choice: we could ignore them or listen to them.

So we prayed about their suggestion in earnest and determined that their vision was real. In March 1978, Lawndale Community Church held its first service with barely more than a dozen people present. I was declared pastor. Since then several churches and denominations have offered to grant me ordination, but I've politely declined, explaining that the blessing I got from the grass roots of Lawndale was all the ordination I need or want.

Knowing that starting a church was the right thing to do did not mean that Anne and I felt prepared. For Anne, living in the city was one thing, but being a pastor's wife was quite another! Even before the first service, feeling insecure about being the only adults in the church, we contacted other ministry-minded couples to see if they would be willing to join us. High on our list were Art and Linda Jones. They were already living in the city, just two miles east of us, while Art attended the University of Illinois Medical School. We also asked Mike and Debbie Stracco, classmates of mine at Wheaton who were living in the Chicago area, if they would come to Lawndale, even if just for a year or two, to help get Lawndale Community Church off the ground. Both couples agreed and were there in the little storefront space below our apartment for the very first service.

A couple months later, one of our first formal acts of outreach as a church was to listen to the community tell us about the needs of the neighborhood. We gathered around a chalkboard and began to make a list: health care, education, jobs, housing, recreation, combating violence and drugs. Anything anyone could think of made the list.

Then I asked, "Is there anything on this list that we can actually do?"

A woman raised her hand and said, "What about the need to have a safe place to do laundry?"

"Maybe the church could get an old washer and a dryer," someone else suggested. "We could put it here in our little storefront so people could come to our church to do their laundry."

I nodded, but inside I was shaking my head no. Though I wanted to offer an encouraging response, I was actually thinking, *Did I really spend four years at Wheaton College to come to Chicago and start a Laundromat?*

Much to my chagrin, however, everyone else thought the idea had possibilities. I resorted once again to my evasive response: "Let's pray about it." And once more I learned the truth of the old adage: Be careful what you pray for, because you just might get it.

A few days later I got a call out of the blue from someone in the suburbs who said to me, "I understand you've got a little urban ministry going on down there that would like a washer and dryer. Well, we have a perfectly good washer and dryer to offer you, because we changed the color scheme in our utility room. So would you be interested?"

I told him we were very interested but had no way of getting them to Lawndale. Not to be denied, this man rented a truck and delivered the machines right to our door.

As strange as it sounds, this was a pivotal event in the history of Lawndale Community Church. This single washer and dryer established a threefold pattern for everything we would do in ministry. The first step was to listen to the *people.* It was the people's idea to start a Laundromat, not Wayne Gordon's. In fact, I didn't want to do it. The second step was *prayer.* We told God about our need and had faith that he would respond according to his will. The third step was *partnership.* After the Holy Spirit laid it on the heart of someone to offer what we needed, we reached out to form a partnership. This process became familiar to us as the Three Ps: People, Prayer, and Partnership.

So we opened that Laundromat, and people came to our storefront church to use it. I remember Donna Holt coming over to use it as a little girl. We put out a little box and asked people to throw in a quarter, a dime, or a nickel if they could. Everything we got went into the church offering on Sunday. For those who had no money, we had a list of jobs they could do in exchange for using the machines: vacuuming, folding paper, stuffing envelopes.

One woman, Judy Kirkland, who still attends our church, came twice a week to do her laundry and was such a good worker that she would finish all the jobs and have nothing left to do. One day she came in and asked, "Coach, do you have a book I could read?"

I remember giving her *The Hiding Place* by Corrie Ten Boom, several books by John Perkins, and other books from my library. She went through about one book a week. This, I thought, was more like the ministry for which I had prepared.

Many times through the years, we have repeated this process of assessing both the community's needs and our ability to respond. On some occasions, the whole community, not just our church, has taken part. Whether the vision is to start a business or to build a housing development, the process remains the same. The idea needs to come from the people. We need to pray for God's help. And we need partnerships to make it happen.

When we gathered around the chalkboard for the first time, the vision of the people of Lawndale was not limited to a washer and dryer. In fact, there were many suggestions offered concerning what we could actually do for the community. Since Art Jones was at the meeting, someone nominated him to start a medical clinic. And knowing that I was a coach, someone suggested that we make a small addition to our weight machine: a whole gymnasium to go with it! These visions, we figured, would take a little longer than procuring a washer and dryer.

We were able to address several of the community's immediate needs, however, by increasing our ministry efforts among the youth. We worked with recent graduates of Wheaton College who were willing to commit to the church for a year or two. I assigned them to high schools to volunteer as tutors or coaches and to start Bible studies. One young man named Steve Heaviland ended up spending seven years with us during the 1980s. He started with a single Bible study at Marshall High School and eventually became youth pastor on the church staff. As we built our youth ministry it was not unusual to get thirty or so high school students in Sunday school.

The vision to build a gym and a health center stayed with us. Then in 1982, a three-thousand-square-foot building that formerly housed an automotive parts store went up for sale two doors down from the church. Before long Cy, a Jewish man from suburban Skokie whose family had run the business for forty-five years, approached me and said, "You know, you're doing great things with the people around here. I'd like to sell this building to you." Cy gave me a figure of $18,000, which was a great price for this building, since it was in pretty good shape. I told him I'd talk to the church board and get back to him. But before I could give him a formal reply, Cy called and said, "We really want you to have this building. I'll sell it to you for $10,000."

Now, if $18,000 was a great price, $10,000 was unbelievable. I went back to the board, and we began dreaming about all we could do with this building. In addition to giving us more space for the present, it gave us some room to expand. We voted unanimously to buy the building.

One indication of our level of sophistication back then is the fact that none of us had thought to ask how much money we had in our bank account before taking a vote. For some reason, I was certain we had at least $10,000. But upon examining the checkbook, I discovered we had just $6,000.

We had previously made a commitment never to borrow money to do ministry, so going to the bank was not an option. I was disappointed, hurt, discouraged, and confused, because in my heart I was convinced God wanted us to have this building. I told our board members the bad news. "You know what?" I said. "I've been going around for a long time telling people that God's plans never lack God's provisions. And we've never not done something because we didn't have the money to do it. I believe we're supposed to buy this building, and I'm very surprised we don't have enough money here to do it."

The next day I called Cy and explained that our board had voted to buy his building only to discover that we didn't have enough money. I didn't tell him how much we had, but I told him I would never dream of asking him to come down any further in the price. I concluded by saying that if the building was still available by the time we raised the additional money, we definitely wanted it.

I'll never forget his response. "Doggone it," he said, "I want you to have that building." He hemmed and hawed for a minute and then asked, "Well, could you come up with six thousand dollars?"

I said to him, "Cy, that's exactly how much money we have."

Since this was a family decision, he said, "Well, let me talk to my wife, and I've got to talk to my mother-in-law." And then he said, "Ah, forget them. I'll sell it to you for six thousand dollars."

The following week, at a board meeting of the Fellowship of Christian Athletes, I was telling the story of how we got this building for $6,000. A businessman whose heart was touched mailed a check the next day in the amount of $10,000, enough to reimburse us for the cost of the building and to pay for some renovations to boot.

We cleaned the building, did some painting, put up a basketball hoop—and we played. The ceiling was just thirteen feet high, and the floor twenty-three feet wide. Water leaked under an old garage door, making the concrete floor even more slippery than it was dry. Still, we played. One young man even slipped and broke his arm one night, but no one ever complained.

We carpeted a spare room in the new building and moved the weight machine into it. The renovations cost about $2,000. So for a total of $8,000 we had a beautiful facility, which we called the Lawndale Community Church Recreation Center.

Isn't it amazing the mileage you can get from one washer and dryer?

Six

Healing the Sick

BACK IN THE LATE 1970s in Lawndale, when people had sore throats or other ailments, they would track down Art Jones after church. Art was in medical school at the Chicago campus of the University of Illinois, and the people of Lawndale Community Church thought that he would be the perfect person to start a medical clinic as a ministry. I thought so too. But one key person was not so certain: Art Jones.

I had become friends with Art before the formation of Lawndale Community Church. He and his wife, the former Linda Lott, were Anne's schoolmates at Taylor University. Art's dream was to serve as a medical missionary overseas. So when he and Linda left for a short-term mission trip to Africa in the summer of 1978, we thought their time in Lawndale had come to an end. But God had other plans.

I spoke with Art after his return from Africa and asked him how things went. "It was a great experience," he said, "but while I was there it seemed like God was tapping me on the shoulder and saying, 'Look around. I don't have that hard a time getting Christian doctors to come to Africa. But you know what? Not too many want to go to the inner cities of America.'"

When Art then told me that God was calling him to start a medical clinic in Lawndale, my heart leaped. I asked him if he was certain.

"One hundred percent," he said.

As Anne and I were expecting our first child in 1980, we began thinking about finding a bigger apartment. We approached Art and Linda about becoming co-owners with us of an apartment building, and they agreed. Together we bought a three-flat. We moved there in September, about the time Angela, our daughter, was born. Art and Linda moved into their apartment the following month, and a woman from church named Mary Rhodes moved into the third unit.

With Art's vision firmly in place, the church began dreaming about finding a bigger building to house the medical clinic. We knew if we put it in the recreation building, the clinic would have no room to grow. Then we thought of an old, dilapidated Cadillac dealership that had closed ten years before. It was on Ogden Avenue, just across the street from where we were holding church services. For a time the Salvation Army had operated a little thrift store in the space, but that had since closed.

For a long time I'd had my eye on that building and the vacant lot beside it, mostly because of its perfect location. I would walk around the land at night and pray that God would give it to us. I told the kids from the church to pray over that land every time they passed by it because someday, I was convinced, it would house our medical clinic, our gym, and a larger worship space to accommodate the church's steady growth.

So as a fellowship, we began to pray about the building. We put out a little basket for people to contribute toward its purchase. By that time, suburban churches were beginning to hear about the budding miracle in Lawndale, and since their contributions were enough to cover the operating expenses of our church, every penny given by church members could go into the bank as seed money for the land we wanted. In

ART

one year we raised $15,000. That combined with an outside gift of $10,000 gave us $25,000 with which to negotiate with the Salvation Army. The price was $35,000 for both the land and the building. They agreed to take $25,000 at that time and the rest a year later at no interest.

The transaction took place in May 1983. At 20,000 square feet, this building could easily house a health center, a gym, and a worship area. We planned to do all three but knew it would entail major renovations. So on the Sunday after buying the building, we held a prayer service during which we laid hands on the building and asked the Lord to bless our efforts.

We developed a brochure to share our vision with people in the broader community. It juxtaposed a picture of the dilapidated building, broken windows and all, with the details of our vision for what that building could become. A friend of the church named Dennis Boothe from Webber Graphics printed up 10,000 copies at no charge.

Later in 1983 we formed a board of directors for the Lawndale Christian Health Center, and early in 1984 we officially incorporated. As Art oversaw the details I renewed my acquaintance with a former classmate at Wheaton College, Janice Steinhouser, who had gone on to become a physician. Janice began attending the church as she made plans to move to Lawndale. She would later become the first physician at our medical clinic while Art finished a fellowship in cardiology at the University of Chicago.

Concerned that we weren't going to have enough money to renovate the building, Art began moonlighting, doing extra work in emergency rooms and depositing the money in the bank. His dedication and hard work inspired and encouraged everyone who shared this vision with him.

Not long after we bought the building, I spoke to a small church group at Winnetka Covenant Church in the suburbs.

This group of about fifteen had formed out of a concern to address the needs of the world's poor. Afterward a man named Bruce Johnson approached me. He said that, as an architect, he would be willing to help us design a building that would house the health center, gym, and church.

The next week, Bruce came to look at the building, which had holes in the roof big enough for cars to fall through. The building had been condemned. Our local alderman pleaded with us to tear it down. Various contractors had told us it was beyond restoration. They advised us to knock it down and start from scratch. But we did not want to do that. For this building, pictured in all its ugliness in the brochure we had sent out to the community, had became a symbol of what God does in human lives. As 2 Corinthians 5:17 puts it, "All things are made new in Christ."

We were aware that the world had given up on the people of North Lawndale. The justice system had given up. Parents had given up. Tragically, many had given up on themselves. But God, we knew, gives up on no one. He is in the business of making people new creatures in Christ. If God could do that with people, maybe he could do that with this old building.

Bruce examined the structure and found possibilities where others had found only despair. A couple of days later he brought in some sketches, and as we looked at them it became clear to me that Bruce was dreaming right along with us. He showed us where we could put the worship area and the medical clinic. He pointed out where the gym might go but said there was not enough height, so we might have to "go down." Before he got too far along, I told Bruce I had no idea how we could pay him. But he quickly replied that money was not an issue. He had some time and he wanted to help.

With the people and the plan for renovation in place, the only challenge that remained was coming up with the money. That challenge was fast becoming a familiar one at Lawndale. One morning a friend of mine came to church and, after the service, quietly put a check in the offering box. The person counting the money came to me and said there must be some mistake. The check was for $25,000, by far the biggest we had ever received. Then the businessman who had previously given us $10,000 to pay for our other building wrote us another check for $25,000. About $10,000 more came in from other sources. With a total of $60,000 in the bank, we were ready to do the renovations.

Then came the estimate on our roof, which took the wind out of our sails in a big way. The lowest appraisal was a whopping $90,000—for the roof alone! Since I had hoped we could do the entire project for $60,000, I was heartbroken.

But then I realized something: since most of the cost of the new roof was in getting rid of the old one, I thought we might be able to help ourselves. So we went out and bought a big saw for $1,000, the kind with wheels that tears through old roofing. And in the spring of 1984, thirty high school kids from North Lawndale gave up their spring break to help Steve Heaviland and me take off the old roof. Don Church took off the entire month of June to help. We worked from dawn till dusk every day. It was like an old-fashioned Amish barn raising, as women from the church made sure we had plenty to eat and drink. The roofing company returned and revised the estimate downward to $30,000. In other words, the sweat of the people of Lawndale was worth $60,000!

During this time Art submitted a grant proposal to the Chicago Community Trust, a local charitable foundation, hoping to acquire funds for the medical clinic. He was asking for a total of $150,000 ($50,000 a year for three years) for operational support. Our optimism grew when we heard they were sending someone out for an on-site inspection.

A woman named Mary paid us this visit. From my perspective, things did not go well at all. First, I had not thought to put on a shirt and tie. When she arrived, I was up on the roof working with the kids. When I shook her hand, I was covered with sweat and tar from head to toe. Second, and more significantly, she pointed out that the health center had not yet received proper status as an official organization and that the Chicago Community Trust had a policy against awarding grants to churches. Not only did she reprimand me for that but she added, "And you'd better get some hard hats on these kids before somebody gets hurt."

That night I was disappointed, but had no one to blame but myself. I said to Art, "I think I blew it, buddy." He was polite, but not very happy with me.

Three or four days later Mary called from the Chicago Community Trust. She said they were not interested in making a contribution in accordance with our proposal. But, she added, they were interested in doing something even better: instead of giving us $150,000 over three years, they wanted to give it all to us up front. The foundation would make an exception and give money to the church, she explained, so long as the church would commit to using the money for the health center only.

What an amazing phone call! Later I asked her why they decided to do this. She replied, "Never in all of our years have we seen a grassroots community effort make something like this happen. When we learned that thirty high school kids had donated their spring breaks, we wanted to do all we could to help you." She again reminded me about the hard hats but said that was a small investment in light of the fact that these kids had earned us a $150,000 grant!

As we proceeded with plans to open the health center Art Jones conducted a demographic study of the community. He discovered that the "crisis level" in Lawndale was seven times higher than the level that had been established by the federal government as acceptable, based on the physician-to-population ratio. And at twenty-nine deaths per thousand, our infant mortality rate—a prime indicator of health conditions—was worse than in many Third World countries. This information enabled us to appeal to additional foundations for assistance.

ANTHONY FRANKLIN

While we were building our medical clinic and gym we needed a night watchman, because we were having a problem with disappearing tools and building materials. Anthony Franklin, who had played football and wrestled for me at Farragut High School, and his friend, Elijah Johnson, known as E. J., volunteered for the job. We set up a makeshift apartment in the building for them to sleep in. Since the roof was like a sieve, when it rained Anthony usually got wet, but he owned with pride the task of protecting our building, even though he did not make a dime doing it.

One summer night I was awakened from a deep sleep when I heard a pounding on my front door. It was Anthony. He informed me that someone was up on the roof, carting away all of our rolled roofing. I called the police and then went to investigate. Anthony could see the guys who were doing it, and he recognized them. They lived in a house just three doors away.

I was furious. First, I do not like being awakened at 2:00 A.M., and, second this was not the first time something had been stolen from the building site. So when I saw the thieves on the street, I started yelling at the top of my lungs for them to give us back our roofing. One of them finally said, "Coach, we didn't think we were stealing from you, man. We thought we were stealing from that roofer guy." I explained in heightened tones that we were the ones who

would be hurt, since we would have to replace anything
that got stolen.

Somehow a stranger by the name of Joe Ball had ended
up in Lawndale that night. He was sitting on a front stoop,
talking with some friends. He did not know me from Adam
and did not appreciate a white man screaming at a group of
African Americans, regardless of the circumstances. So Joe
started cussing me out, telling me I was as good as dead. I'll
never forget Anthony—my football player and wrestler—
stepping in front of his former coach to explain to Joe that
nothing would be happening to me that night.

Finally the police arrived, as did our state representative,
Art Turner, who lived nearby. The police grabbed the two
guys who'd taken the roofing material, after Anthony
pointed them out. The cops took them off to jail but made
no attempt to get back our roofing.

As we headed for home Joe kept following us, continu-
ing his pronouncement that I was a dead man. Finally another guy emerged from the house where they had taken
our rolled roofing and told me not to worry about Joe. I told
him I just hoped we could get our roofing back, adding that
if they returned it, I'd do my best to get his buddies out of
jail. Before long some other guys emerged from the house,
carrying out six rolls of roofing.

I was ready to go, but Anthony and E. J. stood their
ground. They told these guys, "There were seven."

Finally the last one came out. Art Turner and I went
down to the police station and told them we did not want to
press charges. Using Joe's threat against me as leverage, we
told the watch commander that my life could be at stake,
and he finally agreed to let the two thieves go. What is more,
this urban pastor and state representative ended up giving
these guys a lift home. That's kingdom living—urban style.

Today Anthony Franklin is like a son to Anne and me.
We have warm memories of his wedding day several years
ago. He and his wife, B. J., live right across the street from us
and are the proud parents of two children. Anthony continues to greet all who enter our church and medical clinic. I
never heard from Joe Ball again. And the roofing is up
where it belongs—on the roof!

X X X

As money came in the renovations began. High school kids joined me and others from the church to do whatever we could. Elijah Johnson (E. J.), Anthony Franklin, Edward Daniels, William Blackburn, and others worked almost every day for many weeks without getting paid a cent.

Just as in Jesus' ministry, the first public event in our new facility was a wedding, held on Saturday, September 15, 1984—on a concrete floor. Daphine Nesby and Andrew Moore, who had been a part of the church from the beginning, began their life together that day.

Meanwhile local excitement about the health center grew. The kids canvassed the community, putting fliers inside nearly 10,000 doors to announce a health fair that was to be held on September 22, 1984. It would be the inaugural event of the Lawndale Christian Health Center, of which Art was director and I was president of the board.

About 250 people came to the health fair, and all who were sick—about 50 people—got appointments to see Janice the following week in one of our five spanking-new examination rooms. We declared our motto to be: "Quality, affordable health care in an atmosphere of Christian love." During its first year of operation, the Lawndale Christian Health Center had about 4,000 patient visits.

Before the center opened, many people from the Lawndale community who could not afford to pay fees at other medical facilities typically waited ninety days to see a doctor for nonemergency treatment at Cook County Hospital. So early on we established a payment policy that recognized not only the financial limitations of our clients but also their dignity.

Getting something for free tends to strip away a person's dignity. So after doing a substantial amount of research, we instituted a sliding scale of payment based on family size and income. We set the minimum fee at five dollars per visit, as compared with thirty dollars at other clinics in the city. Today, the minimum fee is eight dollars, as compared with an average in excess of fifty dollars elsewhere.

For those who cannot afford five dollars, we have a long list of jobs that need to be done. We charge fifteen minutes of work per visit. Obviously, we apply common sense. Someone who is very sick or bleeding does not have to meet the work requirement. But the truth is that most people want to work. They want to give something in return for what they have received.

Another way we save patients money is by having a drug dispensary on the premises. Because we distribute at cost, they get for about two dollars what would cost ten or twelve dollars at a local drug store. In addition to treating patients, our doctors and nurses regularly ask them if they would like to pray. They leave our health center knowing that they are genuinely loved.

As more people began to use the health center we outgrew the building sooner than we had expected. So in 1992 we expanded by building an addition. Again the people from the community donated their labor.

By this time we had begun to think more creatively about moving beyond the mere treatment of illness and into the area of preventive care. How, for example, could we help a young woman avoid an unwanted pregnancy the first time around instead of the second? We applied for and received federal funds to enable us to hire social workers, case managers, and counselors. One of our counselors goes into the public schools of our community to promote abstinence as the best method of birth control.

Case managers follow up on people who miss a doctor's appointment. We have counselors who specialize in treating drug and alcohol abusers. We have an AIDS prevention and treatment program that includes free AIDS testing. The health center offers classes and seminars on such topics as parenting, weight loss, and breaking the smoking habit.

TOM MOORE

Carrie Moore attended the first Mother's Day service at Lawndale Community Church in 1978. She did not bring along her husband, Tom, who never came to church. He had been in a car accident, was partially disabled, and was searching for some kind of purpose in life. Carrie kept Tom informed about the work being done on the building that would one day house our medical clinic.

"Tom," she told him one day, "you ought to go down there and help out."

So he did. Leg brace and all, Tom worked all day, pulling the nails out of lumber so it could be used again. He also tapped bricks to take off the mortar so they could be reused. He became a regular at the work site.

As trustee board chairmen across the land know, sometimes you can get people who attend church to do some work. But Tom Moore is living evidence that you can also get someone who works to come to church. Every once in a while I would mention to Tom how nice it would be to see him in church.

He would say to me, "Coach, I'm not promising you I'll be there Sunday, but when I come, I'll never stop coming."

I'm sure he told me that at least a dozen times.

Then one Sunday in 1984, guess who walked into church totally unexpectedly? And I'm happy to report that Tom Moore proved to be a man of his word. He committed his life to the Lord and has served the church in many ways, including on the outreach council. I could count on my hands the number of times in eleven years he has missed church.

x x x

We teach prenatal classes and have incentive programs to ensure that young women come for their prenatal visits. We discovered that many young women, after becoming pregnant, would apply for welfare simply so they could see a doctor. Then they had to find a doctor, get a pregnancy test, and make an appointment. Typically this process takes ninety days—during the most crucial prenatal period.

Art Jones requested permission from the state to place a doctor in the Public Aid office. When that was granted, the local United Way chapter gave us money to open a little medical office in Public Aid, particularly for young women. Our doctor would administer the pregnancy test on-site. And we found a way to cut through the red tape so that we could accomplish in less than seventy-two hours what used to take seventy-two days.

Among the most important ministries of the Lawndale Christian Health Center is a treatment program targeting drug and alcohol abuse. If Satan uses materialism and affluence to destroy people in the suburbs, he uses drugs to destroy them in the city. Obviously, the problem of drug abuse has spiritual and psychological dimensions. But it also has a medical dimension. The health center has helped people kick their habits in a variety of ways—from going "cold turkey," which produces horrendous physical side effects, to more gradual approaches afforded by such drugs as methadone. Assessments are made on a case-by-case basis, depending on the person and the substance being abused.

The church community's experience with a woman named Reba Charles first inspired us to do more in the area of substance abuse. Reba was a single mother of two who was addicted to both heroin and alcohol. Her daughter, Chelsea, was active in several of our church programs. Chelsea came to church every Sunday, but Reba never came.

Chelsea cared not only for herself but for her younger brother, Corry.

Every time I saw Reba, she was strung out on something. She'd lost a lot of weight and seemed headed for self-destruction. I crossed paths with her one day about half a block from the church. I grabbed her by the arms and said, "Reba, you tell me how I can help you. I'll do anything to get you off of this." I told her that with Christ's help and with the resources of our medical clinic, we could lick this thing.

Several months later Reba came to me and said she was ready to get off drugs. She searched out a methadone clinic in Chicago, and slowly but surely she kicked her heroin habit. I told her that if she allowed Jesus Christ to become the center of her life, she could conquer alcohol too. She said she wanted to do that and began coming to church.

Reba did not have a job. After a fire destroyed the building where she lived, she and her children had no permanent place to stay. I told her that if she would quit drinking, put on a dress, and get cleaned up, maybe she could earn some money doing things for the church, but first she had to prove herself as a volunteer.

I'll never forget the morning she came to the church all dressed up, ready to work. She looked absolutely beautiful, like a totally different person from the one I remembered as being strung out on drugs. And there was a bounce in her step that wasn't there before; she was excited. Her first job was to hit the buzzer that allowed people to enter the building. She moved on to other things. After a few weeks Reba and I agreed that she would give twenty hours of her time to the ministry in exchange for living rent free in a four-room apartment in one of our church buildings.

Reba kept her part of the deal. She came to church every Sunday and then started coming to Bible studies and other church activities. Today, about four years after she decided to change, she continues to walk with the Lord. She is off welfare. She serves the church by keeping our buildings immaculately clean and has recently begun learning some computer skills.

We now have a Christian twelve-step program for those struggling with drug and alcohol addiction. Led by Leo Barbie of our health center staff, about thirty people meet every evening to support and pray for one another. And the previously mentioned Hope House is a place for men to live and find support during their time of recovery.

All the ministries related directly or indirectly to the Lawndale Christian Health Center are outgrowths of people of vision in this community. The medical and social services represent a commitment to a holistic approach to ministry. We started with five exam rooms and one doctor. Today we have thirty-three exam rooms, twenty doctors, a full-time dentist, and a few volunteer dentists. This year we expect to treat some 60,000 people. As of this writing, the medical center employs about a hundred people, including nurses, lab technicians, clerical support staff, social workers, and case managers.

The sheer size of the medical staff has admittedly made it difficult for us to continue to feel like a family. We've tried to address this by holding a short time of prayer and praise each morning for all staff and by getting together twice a month for Bible study. All of our medical staff members are fully committed to the Lawndale vision. People who come to the health center know they are loved.

As far as I know, ours is the largest Christian health center dedicated to meeting the needs of the poor in America. As of 1992, the infant mortality rate in Lawndale has gone from twenty-nine deaths per thousand down to just under thirteen, only slightly higher than the national average.

Some things haven't changed. Art Jones is still the executive director, as he was from the beginning. Janice
Steinhouser, our first doctor, is now Janice Rossbach, and she
has two children. But she still lives half a block away from
the clinic and walks to work each day. Bruce Johnson is still
designing buildings for us. I would estimate that he and his
partner, Duane Rowe, have donated over half a million dollars' worth of architectural services in the last thirteen years,
without ever charging us a dime.

The biggest change is in the lives of the people of this
community. Thousands of them come each month to seek
healing and in so doing encounter the greatest Healer of all.

Seven

Digging Deeper

FROM ITS VERY BEGINNING, those who started Lawndale Community Church recognized how crucial a role a gymnasium could play in our efforts to befriend and minister to the youth of this community. In the suburbs a nice gymnasium is a common convenience. In the city it is a rare luxury. Far more than a place for teens to stay out of trouble, a gym is where young people not only have fun but discover community and a sense of belonging.

In 1985, with our health center up and running smoothly, our efforts began to turn toward building our gym. Once again we faced the problem that results from combining big dreams with no money.

Fortunately, the first step toward building a gym required little in the way of finances. To get the right ceiling height for our gymnasium, all we had to do was dig a hole 6 feet deep, 125 feet long, and 50 feet wide. Trust me, that is one mighty big hole!

A concrete contractor named Alex Zera, who had done much of the concrete work on our medical center at no charge, gave us a jackhammer and a few wheelbarrows. He sent his sons, Tim and Chris, to teach us how to use the jackhammer. With that, and a dozen or so picks and shovels, we were on our way.

Every day after school, the kids came to dig (and dig and dig) with picks and shovels. They hauled it away in wheelbarrows. Youth groups from suburban churches came in to dig on Saturdays. Anthony Franklin coordinated the effort and worked most days himself. For nine straight months during 1985 we dug almost every day except Sundays. Our herculean efforts even attracted some media attention from local newspapers, which led to some unexpected donations.

One day Alex brought down one of his brothers, who worked for a company that owned a Caterpillar tractor. They absolutely could not believe that the hole they saw before them had been dug by hand. The company ended up lending us the Caterpillar, and in three days the hole was finished.

Then in January 1986 Alex Zera and his crew came down to put in a concrete slab. The very next day we put up a portable basket. Now when kids came after school, they played basketball for an hour or so and then carried concrete blocks to the areas where bricklayers would be working the next day.

Eventually we put in a second basket so we could go full court on that concrete floor, unsure if we would ever be able to afford a wood floor to go over it. We had locker rooms, but they too were unfinished due to lack of funds.

Little did we know, however, that we had some Bears working on our behalf. These were not ordinary bears; they were Chicago Bears who had just won the Super Bowl. All-pro middle linebacker Mike Singletary and his wife, Kim, knew about what we were doing in Lawndale and had even come to the church a few times. Pat McCaskey, a part owner of the Bears and also a good friend, had known about our ministry from the beginning and served on our advisory board. The Bears, we heard, had a few chuckles over those crazy kids down in Lawndale who dug out a gym by hand.

RANDY

One day Kim Singletary called to tell me she had been talking with Pat McCaskey about what the Bears' wives could do for their yearly charity event. They had decided to raise money to help us finish the gym. She asked how much it would take, and I put the estimate at $40,000, which would cover the plumbing, a wood floor, glass backboards, and locker-room furnishings. Kim said she didn't know if they could raise quite that much but said they were willing to give it a try.

MARY RHODES

When Art and Linda Jones and Anne and I decided to buy a three-flat building together, Mary Rhodes agreed to live in the third apartment. Like most people in our church, Mary was not a "big giver." I'm sure she gave ten percent of her income, but that amounted to perhaps thirty dollars a month. As a senior citizen, she lived frugally and saved what she could. She lived on a fixed income, and fixed pretty low at that.

In the days when our gym was a penniless dream, Mary was a good observer. She knew that for the high school youth of Lawndale, digging a massive hole for a gym was a major step of faith. After all, we did not know for certain when—or even if—we would come up with the money to actually build one. But Mary saw those kids digging, day in and day out, and was inspired.

One day I heard a knock on the door of the apartment. It was Mary Rhodes. She reached out to hand me an envelope. "Here, build the gym," she said and immediately walked back upstairs to her apartment.

I opened this envelope to find a money order in the amount of $1,000. Reminded of the biblical account of the widow's mite, I could not help but start to cry. This is the kind of faithful sacrifice that built our gym. This is the spirit of the people of Lawndale.

--- ✗ ✗ ✗ ---

Before long the Bears' wives oversaw the publication of *The Souper Bowl Cookbook*, featuring photos of the families of every player, coach, and front office staff person, along with their favorite recipes. They sold these cookbooks for ten dollars at various retail outlets and at all Bears' home games through the 1986 season, during which the Bears were defending Super Bowl champions. It cost five dollars to produce each book; the other five was designated for our gym.

We proceeded with the work based on Kim's reports on how sales were going. I remember telling the plumber to go ahead with the job and the Bears would pay him later. Then it became apparent that we would have enough for a new gym floor and also for first-rate, high-quality glass backboards. After all that had happened to make this dream a reality, we were determined not to skimp on the backboards!

We held the celebration ceremony for our new gym on April 30, 1987—one of the most rewarding days of my life. Several Bears representatives came to Lawndale, including President Mike McCaskey, to see firsthand our new gym floor and glass backboards. We put up a volleyball net and had a game between the Bears and the Lawndale staff. Our architect, Bruce Johnson, proved he had other talents by beating Mike Singletary at Ping-Pong. The evening also featured the Jesse White tumblers, well known in Chicago, who donated their time and talents. We charged an admission fee of one dollar a head and were able to raise an additional five or six hundred dollars to help complete the projects that remained.

The focal point of this huge celebration was the Bears' presentation of a check for $42,000, more than enough to take care of all our expenses on the gym.

But the Bears were not finished. For one thing, the volleyball game turned into a tradition. Each spring the players still come down to challenge our staff as a fund-raiser. (Lawndale's "Dream Team" beat 'em in 1995!) Also, in 1989, we got a call from Bears owner Virginia McCaskey, Pat's mother and the daughter of legendary head coach George Halas. Each year she treated the Bears' wives to a nice lunch, and this year she suggested coming down and having lunch in our new gym. This would give the Bears' wives a chance to see the results of their labors.

The Bears' wives boarded a luxury liner bus bound for Lawndale. Instead of eating at a fancy restaurant, they ate in our gym. A woman from our church named Belle Whaley, who ran a ministry to senior citizens in our community, cooked all the food, and church staff served as caterers.

Almost all the Bears' wives came, including Diana Ditka, the wife of Bears coach Mike Ditka. It was another opportunity to celebrate our partnership and to share a little more about our ministry. A few days later Mrs. Ditka called me to say that they were moving to a new house and would be getting new furniture. The Ditkas ended up donating their "old" furniture, which was newer than most of what we had, to the ministry. And Virginia McCaskey decided to use the money she saved by not going to an expensive restaurant to buy a scoreboard to make our gym complete. This year the Bears and Pat McCaskey and his wife, Gretchen, paid to have our gym floor resurfaced.

The story of our gym is one of my favorite stories. But the most important part of the story is not the Bears or the backboards. As with all of our ministries at Lawndale, the story is really about changed lives. Among those whose lives were changed is Randy Brown.

Randy grew up in the neighborhood. He started coming around in 1983 as a senior in high school. He wasn't interested in church and was definitely not interested in Bible

study. But he wanted a place to lift weights and play basketball, even though that was back in the days of our slippery
concrete floor and our thirteen-foot ceiling.

After graduating from high school, Randy kept coming
through the summer. Eventually one of the guys invited him
to our Wednesday night Bible study, and Randy decided to
give it a try. Then he started coming to church on Sunday
mornings. He felt comfortable and welcome there. There was
no pressure on him to be someone he was not.

BELLE WHALEY

A block or so away from Lawndale Community Church
is a ministry to senior citizens called Operation
Brotherhood, which provides food, support, and fellowship
to some two hundred elderly people each day. Belle Whaley
and her husband started Operation Brotherhood in 1970.

I remember Belle once wrote me a letter to say how
happy she was about what our church was doing among the
community's youth. She said she wanted to support our
ministry, and she soon became not just a member of our
church but one of my closest friends. When I needed wise
counsel, I looked no further than Belle Whaley.

We suffered a great loss when one morning in 1990 Belle
was killed at the age of seventy-six by a drunk driver. My
heart was so heavy that I canceled a speaking engagement.

The church had recently bought some land right across
the street from Operation Brotherhood. Someday soon,
when people come to Lawndale they will find a beautiful
park with flowers, benches, some nice rocks and shrubbery,
and maybe even a water fountain. They will also find a
plaque explaining that this park was built to honor and remember a wonderful, godly woman: Belle Whaley.

✗ ✗ ✗

In time Randy began to understand what Christianity was all about. In 1984, he made a commitment to follow Christ. His baptism in Lake Michigan was yet another high point of my ministry. Since then Randy has become like a member of our family. He eats dinner at our home every Wednesday night.

After going off to college, Randy returned to Lawndale to become director of our gym ministry. I cannot imagine anyone better suited for such a leadership position. A skilled athlete, he loves sports, and among young people he's a veritable pied piper. Given his generous disposition, outgoing personality, and warm smile, my guess is it takes the average person less than a minute to realize the positive influence Randy has on youth.

Our gym is in use seven days a week. About thirty-five women use it twice a week for an aerobics class. Some three hundred young people—grammar school through high school age—come during a typical week to play basketball in our programs. We also run men's leagues. Guys from the Chicago Police Department and the Fire Department have been over to play. And each spring we host a public school basketball tournament for the younger kids.

Woven into our programs are times for devotions and reflections. Randy has a gift of being able to tell Bible stories and talk about important things without putting young people off. Part of it is because he has put so much time and energy into building relationships. High school kids who come to church on Sundays know that after church they will pile into Randy's car and go out to Denny's for lunch. Within this context of friendship, sharing Christ becomes a most natural thing to do.

Building our gym was worth every ounce of sweat and every callused hand it cost us. Because of our gym ministry, Randy Brown has become part of the solution in Lawndale instead of part of the problem. And because of Randy Brown and God's grace, I am confident that many others will follow suit.

Eight

A Philosophy of Hope

Serving the People

Go to the people
Live among them
Learn from them
Love them
Start with what they know
Build on what they have:
But of the best leaders
When their task is accomplished
Their work is done
The people all remark
"We have done it ourselves."

—ANONYMOUS CHINESE POEM

The above poem was given to me by one of my heroes and chief mentors: John Perkins. If anyone wants the "Cliff Notes" version of the Lawndale approach to ministry, all I have to do is recite this poem.

When I moved to Lawndale in 1975, I had heard of John Perkins but did not know much about him. As I began reading his books my respect for his ideas and philosophy of ministry grew quickly and immensely.

Out of John's ministry to poor people in Mississippi emerged a philosophy that has come to be called "Christian community development." The movement has given rise to many "Joshuas"—ministry leaders who have put into practice the ideas and principles associated with Christian community development. But John Perkins stands alone as the "Moses" of the movement, and he led by his example.

In reading John's books, I realized that his ideas spoke to the heart of everything I had come to Lawndale to accomplish. So in 1982 I decided to visit him in Mississippi. A few months later, just after we had purchased the building that was to become our health center and gym, he came to Chicago for his first visit to Lawndale. He had asked me to pick him up at the airport. I still remember how nervous, though honored, I felt that someone of his stature would ask me to pick him up.

After I gave him the grand tour of our facilities, he came over to our apartment for lunch. "You're doing just what you ought to be doing," he told me. That affirmation, coming from John Perkins, has carried me through many doubting and discouraging moments.

Within the context of what he called the Three R's, John set forth his ideas on *Relocation, Reconciliation,* and *Redistribution.* Relocation addressed living among the people, as described in the Chinese poem. And John saw Reconciliation across race and class lines as being a prerequisite to genuine progress. Under the category of Redistribution, he addressed the need for the "underclass" to develop skills and businesses so that they might increase—through hard work and industry—their capacity to enjoy the resources God has provided.

Without question, the linchpin of Christian community development in the Lawndale context is living in the community. We are a community church, and we insist that those who come to our church live in our community. We have our own Three R's that address the routes people might take to live here: Relocators, Returners, and Remainers. People from

DEACON WILLIAMS

all three groups may leave Lawndale anytime they wish, but while they are here they must choose to be here.

Having grown up in Iowa, I am a prime example of a Relocator. Relocation must be more than a short-term mission project. It entails adopting the new community as home. Over ten white families have relocated in Lawndale over the years, including Art and Linda Jones. Another of our doctors, Louie Winternheimer, and his wife, Lisa, moved to Lawndale seven years ago. Dale and Reecie Craft came to Lawndale in 1984. Dale teaches at Collins High School, and Reecie works at the Health Center. Dave Doig and his wife, Tami, have lived here for over ten years. After earning a master's degree in urban planning from the University of Chicago, Dave helped us start our development corporation. He is now the deputy commissioner of housing for the city of Chicago, while Tami works in our education ministry. Mike and Karen Trout have also relocated to Lawndale. Mike works with our College Opportunity program; Karen teaches public school.

African-American families and individuals have relocated in Lawndale as well. Carey Casey and his family moved here in 1992 when he became shepherding pastor at the church. Carey's secretary, Wanda Helm, is also a relocator, as are Thomas and Tracy Worthy. Thomas leads our Imani Program, which trains people to get jobs and teaches them how to keep jobs, and Tracy works as a counselor in the Health Center.

The second R stands for Returners, people who grew up in the neighborhood, left, and have come back, in most cases out of a commitment to ministry. Anthony and Marla Peguese have returned, as have Lance Greene and his wife, Cindy. Anthony works as a bookkeeper for ministry partner Perry Bigelow's housing ministry. Lance coaches our ministry's highly successful Kaboomer track team for children ages eight through fourteen. Cindy is involved in our church music program.

Roger Love, after graduating from Taylor University, returned to his home community to teach and coach wrestling at Collins High School, his alma mater. His wife, Tosha, also grew up here in Lawndale. It has not been easy for Roger; he has met with all kinds of obstacles. Within minutes of cashing his first paycheck from Collins High School, he was held up at gunpoint and robbed of five hundred dollars, plus two tickets to the Chicago Bulls' home opener. People told him he was crazy to be here.

Richard Townsell has returned with his wife, Stephanie. Richard was born in the neighborhood and grew up in a housing project, without his father around. He and Stephanie have tremendous minds; both graduated from Northwestern University in Evanston, Illinois. I'll never forget what Richard said to me when he was contemplating coming back to Lawndale after teaching in Evanston for five years. "Coach," he said, "for you to live in Lawndale makes you a hero. For me to live in Lawndale makes me a fool."

And he's right. After all, many in both white and black communities perceive that I have achieved success for doing what I have done as a white man in a predominantly African-American community. Richard could do the exact same thing and still be perceived as a failure in his ethnic community, simply because getting out of Lawndale has been so tightly woven into the definition of success. But he came back anyway to become executive director of our development corporation. Meanwhile Stephanie is considering medical school.

The third R stands for the Remainers, those who have stayed in Lawndale all their lives. This group is, in a sense, the most important group. They are the grass roots of this community. They have a complete, unbroken historical context and have held the fabric of the community together so that the returners have had something to return to.

My administrative assistant, Willette Grant, was born here, grew up here, and went to school here. She has had job offers elsewhere, but she has chosen to stay, as have Edward and Tanisha Daniels, who have been coming to the church since they were children. During his high school years, Edward came to Bible studies even when they were scheduled for 6:00 A.M. Now he is a Chicago police officer, and our community is a better place because of it. He also serves on our outreach board. Tanisha is a dedicated member of our health center staff and the mother of "Little Edward." Pat Herrod is another example of someone who has remained. With unbridled enthusiasm she leads the staff each morning in a short time of singing and prayer to get the day off to a joyous start. She doesn't regard the people she works with at the health center as clients but considers them friends.

Stacey Smith lived here through most of her childhood years and remained a part of the community while attending North Park College on the north side of the city, where she earned a nursing degree. She is now a nurse in our health clinic but is making plans to go on to become a doctor.

About eighty percent of our medical staff, including more than half our doctors, live in the community. We believe in this concept so deeply that we will not allow people to be part of the church who will not make a commitment to living in Lawndale. Of course, we invite people to visit, and people from all over the country have done so. We regularly have people from supporting churches in the suburbs visit us. But if they show up for two or three weeks in a row, either Pastor Casey or I sit down and have a conversation with them.

Over the years, I've had many of these conversations with well-meaning people from the suburbs, in which I politely explain that ours is a community church, not a commuter church. I tell them directly, "Unless you're thinking of moving to Lawndale, I don't think you should come to our church." (We make exceptions for nonbelievers.) Although most people understand, our convictions along these lines have resulted in occasional hard feelings.

PRECIOUS THOMAS

Precious Thomas has experienced the best of times and the worst of times in Lawndale. As a child growing up in the 1950s, she remembers safe and good schools, bakeries, flower shops, bookstores, and sleeping on the back porch with the house doors unlocked and open.

When Lawndale changed, Precious did not. She is a remainer. Lawndale is her home, and she believes that our community can someday become again like it was when she was a child.

For sixteen years Precious taught grades three through eight at schools here in Lawndale. She became a part of Lawndale Community Church as a result of her nephews being active here first. Five years ago when she was looking for a career change, I asked her to come to work for the ministry. As director of operations, she takes care of our business, literally. And because of her experience with and love for children, she also works with our after-school program. In 1992 Precious and her sister, Sandra, moved into a building they had purchased with a little help from the church and hundreds of hours of their own labor, which we call "sweat equity."

Some people will relocate to Lawndale, and others will return after having left. But it is remainers such as Precious Thomas who have steadily and consistently upheld the vision of Lawndale as a place worth loving, a place that, no matter what, is home.

--- ✗ ✗ ✗ ---

A second basic element of Christian community development, Lawndale style, is racial reconciliation. Technically, our church is about eighty-five percent black and fifteen percent white. I say "technically" because those of us who have lived and worked together for so long are in some ways unaware of the differences in hue among us. We are all one in the body of Christ. We are all equal in the kingdom of God. And we are all in this mission together.

This is not to say we are the same. For one thing, the very fact that we are perceived to be different by the world outside our church community makes us different. And we are aware of the cultural differences that can sometimes lead to unintended expressions of insensitivity.

If Lawndale Community Church is nothing else, it is a model for reconciliation in a world that continues to be divided along racial lines in both overt and subtle ways. We have sought to follow the admonition in Ephesians 4 to "make every effort to keep the unity of the Spirit through the bond of peace." Over the years we have had what we call "ebony, ivory, and harmony" meetings, which feature candid discussion between and among the African-American people and the white folks from our church. We attempt to meet head-on any issues or problems that threaten to divide us. Our meetings are patterned after the "vanilla, chocolate, and fudge ripple" meetings at Raleigh Washington and Glenn Kehrein's Rock of Our Salvation Church here in Chicago. Our goal is to talk about and work out misunderstandings among us related to racial differences.

I have encouraged people to read books intended to help us understand one another. At the top of my list are Glenn and Raleigh's book *Breaking Down Walls*; Spencer Perkins' and Chris Rice's *More Than Equals*; and Bill Pannell's *The Coming Race Wars?*

We recognize that all the discussion in the world will not necessarily reconcile us to one another. But whether or not we understand or agree with each other fully, we can be reconciled through Jesus Christ. Indeed, we have been reconciled by his death and resurrection. So we always end these meetings by sitting in a big circle and sharing Communion. Then we get the music going over the loudspeakers, bring out all the kids from the nursery, and celebrate. Usually we eat chocolate marshmallow ice cream, since our church is mostly "chocolate," but with some specks of "marshmallow" added in.

Living in the community and modeling racial reconciliation are both fundamental to Lawndale's philosophy of ministry. But ultimately, Christian community development entails ministries of outreach. Lawndale Community Church has a very specific target area, consisting of a forty-square-block area in the immediate vicinity of the church. Our four-word theme is "Loving God, Loving People" (this comes directly from the Great Command of Jesus in Matthew 22), and our mission is to redeem the Lawndale community.

As our church's prominently displayed vision statement puts it,

> LCC's mission is to redeem the Lawndale community. We seek to bring Christian wholistic revitalization to the lives and environment of its residents through economic empowerment, housing improvement, educational enrichment, quality affordable health care, and Christian discipleship.
>
> LCC envisions a future when Christian values undergird the attitudes and actions of Lawndale's residents; when existing community people are empowered to live in harmony and security; when vacant lots and aban-

doned buildings are converted into new, affordable homes and rehabbed apartments; when the majority of homes are owner-occupied; when high school and college graduation are accepted expectations; when job skills abound; when all people have quality affordable health care; and where Jesus Christ is Lord!

All of our ministries are geared toward encouraging men and women, boys and girls, to put their faith in Jesus Christ and to allow their lives to be governed by the truth of Scripture. But living in Lawndale has helped me realize that simply persuading people to become Christians should never be the only goal of ministry. The first person I helped to become a Christian here could not read. Giving his life to Christ did not instantly make this young man literate. Similarly, people who have had their water or heat shut off have come to Christ through our ministry. But when they go home, they still have no water or heat.

If our love for these brothers and sisters is genuine, how can we ignore their needs to have a decent and safe place to live, to have an opportunity to pursue meaningful work, and to have access to physical healing when they are injured or sick? It is absurd, therefore, even to think in terms of such dichotomies as spiritual versus physical or to try to determine which is more important. Christian community development, virtually by definition, is wholistic ministry that seeks to meet physical, spiritual, emotional, and social needs in the name of Christ, without concern for which is most important.

If people don't have food to eat, we have to give it to them. And if they can't read, we must teach them how. If they don't have jobs, we must help them find work. This is not the "social" gospel; it is the gospel of Jesus Christ, who said, "For I was hungry and you gave me something to eat, and I was thirsty and you gave me something to drink" (Matthew 25:35). We have been called to make disciples of all people. Discipleship is not just about memorizing Bible verses. From a biblical perspective, discipleship is about helping people to be whole, to be restored to the image of God in which they were created.

One of the first things Lawndale Community Church did was to survey our community to find out why people did not go to church. We discovered four basic answers:

1. They felt they did not have nice enough clothes to wear.
2. They had no money to contribute.
3. They were angry or disappointed with God.
4. They felt the church was doing nothing to help the community.

We made a very conscious effort to address all four perceptions.

First, if we have a dress code at our church at all, it is more like a "dress down" code. When I preach you can find me in blue jeans but never in a tie.

We addressed the money concern simply by deciding never to pass an offering plate. Instead we have a box in the back of the church for people who wish to contribute. I have long admired the fund-raising model established by such servants of God as J. Hudson Taylor, the great missionary to China, and George Müller, who ran orphanages in England. They prayed about their needs and told others about what they were doing, but they did not go out and ask for money. We at Lawndale have followed that path. All I have ever done is to tell people about what we are doing and leave the rest to God. We ask for money only when appealing to foundations, which are in the business of giving it away.

The third concern—about being angry or disappointed with God—we addressed directly in our preaching and teaching ministry. In that process, we discovered that most anger with God is based on a misunderstanding of who God is and what, according the Scriptures, God promises and desires of his followers.

We addressed the fourth concern—the issue of how the church serves the community—by making service to this community a central part of our mission.

Even though the concepts of Christian community development may be new to many, the movement is strong and growing. In 1989 about two hundred people met in Lawndale to discuss the possibility of forming some kind of association or fellowship network. I left the room for just a few minutes and returned to find that I had been elected president of the Christian Community Development Association.

CCDA has grown from thirty-seven founding members into an association comprised of over three thousand individuals and some three hundred churches and ministries, representing thirty-five states and over a hundred cities. As our brochure states, "More and more Christians are discovering the simple truth that people empowered by God are the most effective solution for the spiritual and economic development of the poor."

Long before the existence of the CCDA, John Perkins was laying its groundwork by living out its formative principles. Nothing I can write or say can adequately express what I and this movement owe to John, who over the years has not only been my mentor but my friend. He and his wife, Vera Mae, have stayed at our house many times. My children call them Grandma and Grandpa Perkins. Lawndale's tribute came in the form of the John and Vera Mae Perkins

Center. Dedicated in 1994, this building houses a library with books and other resources in the area of African-American history, urban ministry, spirituality, and, of course, Christian community development. It was the least we could do to recognize someone in whose footsteps many have attempted to follow, someone who has inspired us all through his life of sacrifice, integrity, and devotion to Jesus Christ.

Part 3

Christian
Community
Development

Nine

Investing in People

IT DID NOT TAKE me long after moving to Lawndale to recognize that our community suffered from a severe dearth of leadership. Most of those who were considered community leaders—professional people, business people, and schoolteachers—lived outside Lawndale and commuted here to work. Though I tried to persuade proven leaders—black and white—to come to Lawndale, my efforts produced little fruit.

One day I voiced my frustrations to Tom Skinner, who would eventually become a trusted friend and advisor till his death in 1994.

"Wayne," he told me, "you are looking in the wrong places for leaders. The leaders are not outside the community; the leaders are already in the community." Tom challenged me to make a commitment to raise up a new generation of leaders right here in Lawndale.

That conversation changed my entire perspective on leadership development. I began to look at the people of Lawndale, especially the young people, with new eyes, thinking less in terms of who they were and more about the kinds of people they could be if someone would only make an investment in their lives.

The process of leadership development is essentially the process of empowering others. It entails a major commitment of time, money, and energy. Also, those committed to transferring power from their own generation to the next must at some point be willing—and humble enough—to let go, to take a backseat in order to create space for others to make their own marks.

As I got more serious about leadership development I began to examine Scripture in light of the task at hand. I realized that Jesus, in addition to being our Savior, friend, and teacher, was a developer of leaders. Several of his strategies leaped out at me from the gospel narratives, especially Matthew. In Matthew 4:18–22, we find Jesus handpicking his disciples, making an intentional effort to identify those who would become leaders. Those of us who aspire to develop leaders must follow that example by being alert to recognize, and prepared to designate, those who will become leaders.

Then after selecting his leaders, Jesus teaches them (Matthew 5–7). He spends quality time with his disciples, as illustrated by the Sermon on the Mount, in which he sets forth the kingdom principles. Leadership development cannot take place without teaching. The best teaching takes place not formally in a classroom but informally in the context of relationships characterized by mutual respect. We must pick the right times, recognize those "teachable" moments wherein a single statement or lesson can last a lifetime. Those of us who can cite such landmarks in our own lives must recognize our responsibility to impart them to others.

In Matthew 17, we find Jesus choosing a few from the many. He regularly singles out Peter, James, and John to share special experiences with him. They accompany him to the Transfiguration and to the Garden of Gethsemane. We can follow this example in such practical ways as bringing those with the greatest potential for leadership along with us on a speaking engagement, cross-country trip, or camping weekend. We must not be deterred by possible accusations of favoritism, which can reduce us to inaction.

TOMORROW'S LEADERS

In Matthew 20:26–28, we learn from Jesus that "whoever wants to become great among you must be your servant, and whoever wants to be first must be your slave—just as the Son of Man did not come to be served, but to serve, and to give his life as a ransom for many." At one point, Jesus models this servant leadership by getting down on his knees (John 13) to wash his disciples' feet. It is incumbent on us as well to serve those we are attempting to develop. We must guard against the tendency to have them serve us in exchange for the privilege of coming along. A developer of leaders is not a "boss" but a servant capable of elevating the stature and affirming the dignity of those he is committed to developing.

Many, I realize, are more qualified than I to expound on the principles of leadership development. But from my experience here in Lawndale, I have gleaned some principles that may help others who wish to develop leaders:

1. See Fifteen Years into the Future. My rule of thumb is that it takes at least fifteen years to develop new leadership in a community. Some of those who have begun stepping into leadership roles in Lawndale today are young men and women I have known—and thought of as future leaders— since they were freshmen in high school. I have visited them at college, worked with them, had fun with them, counseled them, and officiated at their weddings. If someone asks me what one person can do to build the next generation of leadership, I say start teaching a kindergarten class at church and stay with that same group of kids right on through their college years."

2. Make Them Feel Important. Jawanza Kunjufu, in his book *Countering the Conspiracy to Destroy Black Boys*, quotes a notorious Chicago gang leader (now in prison) as saying, "We will always get the youth because we know how to make them feel important." We need to go out of our way to help our young people realize how important they are, not just in and of themselves, but as future leaders of the church and community.

Sometimes churches tend to push young people aside, tell them to be quiet when they speak up, and make them feel unwelcome in adult church settings. If our children and youth cannot be incorporated into the life of the church, they need special programs of their own. They must have the opportunity to develop a view of their church community as being a place where they feel at home, have fun, and sense that they are contributing to something extremely important.

I cannot emphasize enough how important a pat on the back or a kind word is to a young person. We ought to praise them thirty-five times for every time we criticize them. This is their season of life to be built up, to gain confidence. It is especially important to shower praise on those who come from homes where they may not have received much positive attention.

3. Don't Go Anywhere Alone. Future leaders need to get out into the world, experience its diversity, and become familiar with its problems and its mysteries. So I say take them with you; share your life with them. I try not to go anywhere alone. If I notice some youngster hanging around the office, I'll take him with me to the bank, grocery store, or Laundromat.

I also try not to travel alone. Young people have accompanied me on trips all over the country: Jackson, Mississippi; Detroit; New York City; Washington, D.C.; and elsewhere. For some it was their first airplane trip and also their first exposure to models of successful Christian community development outside Lawndale. Sometimes we pack young folks into a van and travel cross-country. What sounds like a nightmare from an adult perspective is actually a rare opportunity for current and future leaders to build relationships between and among themselves.

4. Be Accessible. Future leaders must know that they are among your highest priorities in life. They must realize that you are available to talk with them or pray with them whenever they need you. Over the years, I have always made sure that people know my home phone number and feel free to stop by the house. They have consistently respected my privacy and my need to have time alone or with my family.

Accessibility must go beyond formal times together, such as Bible studies and other organized activities. Sometimes the agenda for getting together should be no agenda at all. These unstructured times when we can laugh, cry, pray, share deep thoughts, or talk sports, I am convinced, are the times that register the most impact on young lives.

5. Expose Them to Other Role Models. Bring as many lives and collective years of wisdom and experience as possible to bear on building leaders. Tom Skinner, Dolphus Weary, and John Perkins came to the church to preach when we were just a storefront of fifty people. Sometimes a role model from outside the community can accomplish in one poignant illustration or story what formal leadership training cannot accomplish in fifteen years—or can never accomplish at all. Don't just share yourself with others; share others as well.

6. Involve Your Family. When you are ministering to a community in which broken or incomplete families are the norm, whole families must work particularly hard to open their circle to welcome others. We must work at developing a concept of the community—especially the Christian community—as a sort of extended family. Those future leaders who plan to have families of their own gain immeasurably from witnessing models of Christian family life.

The freedom to include others in family life differs, of course, with each family. But I encourage as many intact families as possible to invite future leaders over for dinner on a regular basis and to include them in family activities and vacations. In addition to what these young people learn from discussions and conversations, they will get an inside look at how successful families live and worship, and how parents discipline children.

7. Remember Those Who Are in College. I have never believed that a college education should be a prerequisite to community leadership. In fact, some of our most capable leaders do not even have high school diplomas, and I don't know where we would be without them. One of my commitments through the years, however, has been to see to it that as many young people as possible who have the ability and desire to attend college get the opportunity to go.

It used to be that I thought my task was finished when someone enrolled in college. I realized there was more to it when the first ten people I helped get there all dropped out. I learned that though our young people might be out of sight, they should never be out of mind, particularly if they have no access to a family support system.

Through the years, we have recognized and encouraged our college students in many ways, including by providing financial help. As September approaches we hold a back-to-school dinner. We coordinate a winter retreat in downtown Chicago during semester break. We make sure that all college students have "adoptive families" who send them letters and remember them on their birthdays. The church sends our monthly newsletter so they know what's going on back home. We also send an occasional "care package."

Our college students know they are free to call collect anytime they need to talk with someone. What they don't always know is when I or someone from the church will stop by to pay them a visit just to find out how they are doing.

8. Love, Love, Love. This principle actually undergirds all the others, but I highlight it here because of its supreme importance. Not only do we need to love those we are attempting to empower as future leaders but we need to let them know in no uncertain terms that they are loved. I remember telling one young future leader point-blank that I loved him, and he told me this was the first time he had heard those words from anyone. Not only must we tell others that we love them but we must demonstrate that love through our attitudes and actions.

9. Let Them Fail. Perhaps you have experienced, as I have, the frustration that comes from trying to learn a computer task from some "expert" who does not want to let go. They start by telling you how to do it, but before long their hands are all over the keyboard, the task is done, and you have no idea how it happened. When your so-called teacher's work is done, you are no better off.

Standing by while others fail can be the hardest part of leadership development, but there is no way to avoid it. We must be willing to fight our instincts to intervene. We must risk taking a step or two back in order to assure that the major steps forward will continue into the future. New leaders must at some point be given the opportunity to take over, which means the freedom to make mistakes. Otherwise, just like the computer teacher, we have failed our students.

This does not mean that anything goes. When the reins of leadership are turned over to another, it is always a good idea to establish boundaries. Perhaps those boundaries can be set in terms of budgetary limits, time deadlines, or statements of desired outcome. But again, so long as the new leaders operate within the boundaries, a hands-off policy is essential. I have found it easier as the years go by to let go, especially after being humbled by the realization that sometimes the new leaders have better insights and abilities than the old ones!

We have worked to develop leaders not just among those who were born in Lawndale but among those who have relocated here, including Andy and Debbie Krumsieg. Andy came to Lawndale to work as a carpenter and eventually became the director of our housing ministry.

Despite everything we do to develop leaders with the hope that they will stay, ultimately we emphasize the lordship of Christ. People should not stay in or return to Lawndale because I want them to do so but because the Holy Spirit has prompted them. This is exactly what happened with Lance Greene.

I had known Lance since he was twelve years old, and I had long envisioned him as a potential community leader. In 1988 my son, Andrew, and Anthony Franklin and I borrowed an old van and headed south to visit some of the college students from the church, including Lance. We covered ten states in seven days, visiting such institutions as Alabama, A & M, Taladaga University, and Prairie View A & M (near Houston), where Lance Greene was enrolled. He had no idea we were coming. We found out the number of his dorm room and waited in the lobby. When he walked by, he said, "Hey, Coach" and kept walking. Then it hit him that we were in Texas, not Chicago, and he was joyous.

Then we all buzzed over to Southern Texas University to pick up another young man from the church, went out, and had one great time. Lance was so moved that we had come this far to visit him that he offered me a parting gift. He took something off the wall of his dorm room and said he wanted me to have it as a token of his appreciation. It was a certificate he had received for being an All-American track runner at Prairie View. I told him I didn't want to take it, but he insisted I do so.

After graduating from college, Lance got a good job offer in Dallas. When he was back in Lawndale for his brother's wedding, I figured it might be the last time I would see him for a while. He came to church the day after the wedding. Afterward he told me that during the service the Lord grabbed hold of his heart and said, "Lance, you're supposed to stay here." Lance told me that day, "Coach, I'm going to help build the Lawndale Miracle."

In returning to Lawndale, Lance started a trend among college graduates from our community. He now coaches our community track team (ages eight through fourteen), known as the Kaboomers. It is one of the best track clubs in the nation. We have been state champs, regional champs, and have produced several All-American runners. Because they must have at least a C average in school to compete, Lance helps them with their education as well as with their running. As for Lance's All-American certificate, I display it proudly on my office wall, making sure to explain to anyone who asks that I'm really not that fast. In any case, Lance's story is a perfect illustration how leadership development efforts can lay the groundwork for God's call.

When I was a young man full of energy, I was like most other youthful folks in thinking I could go on forever. But there is nothing like a persistent "spare tire" in my midsection and aching muscles after a late-night basketball game to remind me that I am not as young as I used to be. From my "fortysomething" perspective, I hope I still have many years of ministry left in Lawndale. But I am comforted to know that the torch of leadership is in the process of being passed.

Ten

A Place to Call Home

MILLARD FULLER, FOUNDER OF Habitat for Humanity, likes to tell the story of how, driving around Atlanta one day with a group of people, he pulled up in front of one of the organization's first house-building projects. A friendly looking little boy stood outside the house—a house that former President Jimmy Carter had happened to help build. Fuller rolled down the window of the car and asked the youngster what he thought about his new home. After the boy expressed how happy he was to have a nice place to live in, Millard commented, "You know who helped build that house, don't you?"

The child beamed from ear to ear. "Yes, I do," he said. "My dad did."

In Lawndale we, like Millard Fuller, have discovered that in addition to being a safe and comfortable place to live, a house can go a long way toward providing a sense of pride and dignity. We have long realized that any effort to persuade businesses and people to remain in or move to North Lawndale would have to include providing affordable and desirable places for people to live.

Housing in North Lawndale has gradually deteriorated over the last forty years. Most of the buildings went up between 1900 and 1920 and have fallen into disrepair. Whenever a fire guts a building, which is a frequent occurrence, that building either gets boarded up and abandoned or torn down.

Between 1960 and 1970 North Lawndale lost about thirty percent of its housing stock. This decline was echoed by a drop in population from 120,000 in 1960 to about 65,000 by 1980, which is about where it is today. Most of those who have stayed have done so because they had nowhere else to go.

In our first apartment in Lawndale, Anne and I had a bucket of water freeze overnight. We had no furnace or boiler, just a small stove that served as a space heater. Still, we were better off than many people in our church. One of the most common urban tragedies is a house or apartment fire that results from people simply trying to protect themselves from the cold.

As a church, our first response was to help people fix up the apartments they were renting. We found, however, that after the renovation, landlords—who, of course, lived outside Lawndale—would typically jack up the price. We quickly figured out that if people were going to have decent, affordable housing, our church would have to get more involved.

In about 1985 the church began to buy abandoned buildings at next to no cost. We would fix them up and rent out apartments at rates that were slightly under the market value and way below what slumlords typically charged for something similar. The proceeds from rental income went toward additional building purchases. Over the years we have expanded to the point where today we own and manage about a hundred apartments, charging between $200 and $500 a month in rent.

In 1980, we began to experiment with co-ownership. Families who could not afford to buy a house or apartment

CHELSEA AND REBA

building alone could cut the cost of ownership in half by going in with someone else. This goes against the grain of individualistic American culture, but that did not stop Anne and me from buying a building with Art and Linda Jones. Over the years, several additional families have followed suit.

By the mid–1980s we had determined that the best way to provide adequate housing—and to empower people in the process—was to help them own their homes. We formed the Lawndale Christian Development Corporation as an entity separate from the church, in order to have access to public funds. Incorporated in 1987, our development corporation, now guided by Richard Townsell, oversees several programs related to housing, economic development, and education.

We have bought many an old, abandoned building with the goal of renovating it and selling it at an affordable price. Sometimes we have picked them up at tax sales for $500. And we have taken advantage of a city program that enables organizations such as ours to purchase a building for literally one dollar.

While buying old buildings was easy enough, turning them into places where people could live was a little more complicated. Sometimes it has made more sense to pay a few thousand dollars for a building that might not require too much in the way of renovation. In fact, that is the route we went in 1987 when the church purchased its first building for the exclusive purpose of fixing it up and selling it. We got some help from a parishioner at Christ Church of Oakbrook who was familiar with our ministry and wanted to do something to help. Dr. Art DeKruyter, the church's pastor, brought him in to visit. We looked at a building that we thought would cost us about $25,000 to buy and another $35,000 to renovate. This man ended up giving us $60,000 through Christ Church of Oakbrook in two installments.

The building we wanted happened to be located on South Avers Street, which had been featured in a 1986 *Chicago Tribune* front-page article, based on its status as the number one street in the city for buying and selling drugs. Two of the city's most notorious drug dealers lived on South Avers. It was here that ten Chicago police officers enabled a drug ring to operate in exchange for bribes. South Avers Street grabbed headlines when these officers, known as the "Marquette Ten," were caught and convicted.

The drug ring was still in operation, however, when we purchased the building as the first step of what we called "Project Salt Block." In addition to providing affordable housing, we wanted to begin reclaiming our streets from the drug dealers. What better place to start than at the center of their operation. We wanted to reclaim this block by being salt and light in our community.

We bought our first building on South Avers from drug dealers for $25,000. We used the rest of the money we had been given to renovate it. Then it was time to sell it, and at $60,000 it was a tremendous deal except for one thing: location. No one from our church who could afford to buy the house wanted to live on South Avers because it was so dangerous. Finally Andy and Debbie Krumsieg, after much prayer and thought, decided to be the first. Andy had joined the church staff after graduating from Wheaton College and had been working with the housing ministry, renovating apartments. He and Debbie firmly believed in the project. Once they made their decision, Dale and Reecie Craft decided to join them as co-owners.

Now we had a Christian presence in the heart of drug-dealing territory, and we also had our $60,000 back. Not long after that I received a call from a husband and wife ophthalmologist team who said they wanted to give us some money. I explained that I had just that day been to a scavenger sale and bought an apartment building in the neighborhood for $500. I told them it would cost about $40,000 ($20,000 per floor) to renovate. They told me they wanted to cover those costs.

With that contribution, we had over $100,000 in seed money to continue what we called our Rehab for Ownership program, which today is coordinated by Bernard Harris, a lifelong Lawndale resident. This $100,000 has turned over several times and continues to turn over today as we buy buildings, fix them up, and sell them to people in the community. At this writing, we have ten two-flats in the process of renovation. People get a great deal on a building, and we get our money back to repeat the process.

The reason home buyers get a house or apartment building for a good price is that they provide much of the labor—hundreds of hours of "sweat equity" on Saturdays and after working hours—in order to earn part or all of the down payment. Take my word for it, when these people move into a new or newly renovated home, they know they have not got something for free but something they have earned through a major commitment of time and effort. All the church has done is to create the opportunity for them to own a home where none existed before.

A foundation funds our sweat equity program by contributing $2,000 at closing in exchange for the labor. That is about $1,000 short of what is needed for an average down payment in Lawndale. So we also have a lease-purchase program coordinated with Northern Trust Bank. This program enables people to make part of the down payment on a house after they have moved in. For the first few years, they pay rent, with the understanding that they are planning to buy. We withhold about fifty dollars a month to go toward the down payment. This fifty dollars actually goes to reimburse Northern Trust, because according to the arrangement, they give us the entire down payment up front so that the money is available for our development corporation to use on other projects.

As part of our Rehab for Ownership program, we conduct a series of classes through which people learn what it takes to own a house. They learn how to manage money more responsibly, how to get out of debt, and how to improve their credit rating. They learn what a down payment is and what "points" are. They learn that a "balloon loan" has nothing to do with helium. For people who have rented all their lives, these are foreign concepts. Those who come through these classes together develop a strong sense of camaraderie. And the thirty-five-dollar charge for twenty hours' worth of classes reinforces the notion that nothing comes for free.

Making a down payment is one reason people cannot afford to buy houses. But having addressed that problem, we realized that many cannot afford a mortgage payment either. The only way to address that is to build houses for less money.

The average cost of a house in Chicago is about $100,000. About one-fourth of that goes toward the land, one-fourth for building materials, one-fourth for labor, and one-fourth for interest, fees, and various hidden costs. Around 1990 or so I began to think about how the cost of building a house could be kept to a minimum. Fortunately, suburban home builder Perry Bigelow was thinking about this too and was coming up with some very innovative and creative ideas and models.

One thing Perry helped us understand was that people working together can accomplish a lot more than individuals working alone. In other words, the whole is usually greater than the sum of the parts. Building houses together would also enable bulk purchases of supplies. And we already knew we could get land in Lawndale for next to nothing. The savings in all these areas would in turn limit the amount of interest.

Based on these principles, the Harambee Homes program was born. "Harambee" is a Swahili word that means, in essence, "Let's come together and push." The program consists basically of people building homes together. At this writing, we have one site where eight families are working to build their homes on land donated to us by the city of Chicago, which, of course, has a vested interest in restoring communities.

Of the eight families, four are headed by single mothers. But these women get right out there with everyone else, with hammer and nails and apron. Every Tuesday and Thursday night and all day Saturday, these people are out there working. Experienced builders from the suburbs have donated their time to oversee the project and to do specialized labor. Perry Bigelow has a special incentive to make sure things are done right, since he will be moving into one of the homes. (He relocated to Lawndale in 1993.)

The people have been working on their homes now for over two years. By the time they finish, each family or individual will have put in over a thousand hours of labor. And they will never take their homes for granted.

The Harambee Homes project is just one of the ways we are helping the people of Lawndale own their own homes. We are also a part of the Westside Isaiah plan, a coalition of twenty-two churches that are building new houses at various sites on the city's West Side, including Lawndale. A coalition of seven churches, spearheaded by our development corporation, is building Bethesda Waters of North Lawndale, which will consist of fifty-two new houses on a formerly vacant lot. The model home is already up. Aided in part by the city's New Homes for Chicago program, people will be able to purchase for $50,000 homes that appraise out at $90,000 or more.

Despite everything we were doing in the area of housing, I learned in 1990 through a high school girl from our church that it was not enough. The place in which Chelsea Charles (see Chapter 6) and her mother and younger brother had been living was gutted by fire. It was the second place they had been forced out of because of fire. So Chelsea came into my office one day and said, "Coach, you're helping everybody own their houses. Why can't you help us? We don't even have a place to live."

Her question tugged at my heart. I realized that all our efforts to help people become self-sufficient were aimed at those who had a little something with which to work. But for those who had nothing at all, we had nothing to offer.

As it had been done many times previously, we at the church began to think and to pray about what we could do. As we studied the problem of homelessness we discovered something surprising: many who are homeless can afford to pay rent but cannot save up enough to put down a security deposit on top of that first month's payment.

We began to think of our principles of work, opportunity, and dignity in the context of homeless families. The result was our Samaritan House program. We immediately made a few of the church-owned apartment units available at a monthly rent based on income, with no security deposit required. Those who move in agree to abide by a few rules we established for the program. After three months, we apply their rent payments toward a security deposit on another apartment. If there is anything left over, we buy an appliance or piece of furniture for them. (Often when people are evicted from a home or apartment, their possessions are simply piled by the street, where, of course, everything of value disappears within a few hours.)

In accordance with the rules of the program, we require people to attend church on Sundays and to become involved in at least one growth activity of the church, such as a Bible study or support group. They also have to attend a weekly budgeting class to learn how to manage their resources more efficiently. The goal was to put families and individuals on a track where they would not have to worry about being homeless again.

With this program in place, the church purchased for $15,000 another building that was to become our Samaritan House. One suburban church expressed interest in paying the $40,000 it would take to renovate the building. But though this church's missions committee approved, its board of elders rejected the idea.

Upset and discouraged, I devoted my entire sermon the next Sunday to the Samaritan House. I shared the story of how Chelsea had alerted us to the fact that we were doing little to help the poorest of the poor among us. Although I am greatly appreciative of all we have received from suburban churches, on this occasion I was deeply perturbed. "Since when do we let suburban churches dictate to us the will of God?" I said. "God is calling us to build this Samaritan House to empower people never to be homeless again, and we're going to do it."

That morning, for the first (and last) time, I passed out pledge cards, asking people to commit to giving whatever they could. I told them that if we did all of the work and shopped around for deals on supplies, we might be able to renovate the building for $20,000. I challenged them to give a total of $20,000 over and above their normal giving over the next eighteen weeks and to roll up their sleeves and spend as much time as they could working.

The church people got excited, and that day they pledged the $20,000 for which I had asked. When the eighteen weeks was up, not $20,000 but $23,000 had come in, much of it in wrinkled envelopes on which was crudely scrawled the word "Homeless." I was so proud of our people and their willingness to sacrifice what little they had to help others who had less.

Then there was Kim Beisser, an old friend of mine from Iowa. He donated $2,000 worth of lumber. Andy Krumsieg supervised the work and did a lot of it himself. We completed the job for about $25,000 and did it with almost no help from the outside. This contributed to our own growing sense of empowerment.

We have been operating our Samaritan House program for five years now. Most people stay for just three months and then move on to another apartment. They can apply for extensions, but may not remain in the program for more than six months, and, to provide the incentive for them to move on, we credit only the first three months of their rent toward a security deposit somewhere else.

If people do not have jobs, we try to help them find one during their time in Samaritan House. Or we help them apply for public aid. We are by no means opposed to welfare, as some are. But we view it as short-term assistance to enable people to get back to self-sufficiency.

That has happened with Chelsea and her family. They were the first to move into Samaritan House. They went from there to an apartment. Today they are one of the eight families building their own homes through the Harambee Homes project. And Chelsea is set to graduate in 1996 from Northern Illinois University with a degree in business communications.

One of our ministry goals is to see to it that by the year 2000 no abandoned buildings or vacant lots remain in our target area of forty square blocks. When our Lazarus project, currently under construction, is completed, we will have renovated over 150 apartments. We have owned over a hundred pieces of property, which we have refurbished and sold to families in North Lawndale.

About fifty abandoned buildings and perhaps three hundred vacant lots remain. We plan to fill those vacant lots with parks, playgrounds, and, of course, housing. Despite the successes we have enjoyed, however, let me state for the record that to provide affordable housing is difficult work. It costs a lot of money and occupies a lot of staff. Managing rental units is a thankless task, especially when someone consistently fails to pay rent or violates their lease, requiring us to make tough decisions. Housing, perhaps more than any other urban outreach effort, carries with it the potential to bring a ministry down. Nevertheless, we expect our efforts in Lawndale to result in an increase in the population over the next five years. We think that by 2000 we will have a friendly, attractive little neighborhood of between 10,000 and 12,000 people. There are those who say that for all this to happen would take a miracle. I agree. But at Lawndale, it would not be our first.

Eleven

A Piece of the Pond

MY FRIEND DR. JAWANZA Kunjufu tells the story of a conversation he had one day with a young man in Los Angeles who sold drugs for a living and had a Mercedes to show for it. He asked this young man, "Do you know anybody who's been doing what you're doing for ten years?"

After thinking for a few seconds, the man replied, "I guess I don't."

"Where are they?" Dr. Kunjufu asked.

The man replied, "Well, they're either dead, in prison, or strung out on drugs."

"Don't you think that's probably where you're going to end up?" asked Jawanza, hoping to get the young man to reconsider his source of livelihood.

Instead the man responded, "I'd rather end up like that than go back to where I came from."

This exchange depicts the sense of utter hopelessness that permeates our inner cities. Young people perceive their options in life as ranging from bad to none at all. Of course, there are intelligent, highly motivated young men and women who grow up in the inner city and can basically write their own career tickets. They might even benefit from affirmative action programs.

Unfortunately, affirmative action does not operate at the lower levels of society, where it is most needed. The typical young African-American man of average intelligence and ability will be judged inferior, because he does not know how to speak or act in the majority culture and because he has lacked opportunities for life-enriching and mind-expanding experiences. Even if he sticks it out and graduates from high school, sometimes the most he can hope for is a job that offers minimum wage with a modest benefit package.

If, on the other hand, he drops out of school to sell drugs, he can make more in a day than he could make in an entire week at a minimum wage job. He gets no medical benefits, but the local kingpin might let him drive a fancy car from time to time. All in all, it is a seductive, glamorous lifestyle. Even though it never lasts, in this instant gratification society of ours, it is more than enough to lure our young people who have grown up without a moral compass into drug and gang activity.

Most of us have heard the adage, "Give a man a fish and he eats for a day. Teach a man to fish and he eats for a lifetime." But in a recent speech, Richard Townsell (who heads up our community development arm, the Lawndale Christian Developement Corporation) suggested that genuine economic empowerment goes one step beyond teaching someone to fish. It also addresses the question of who owns the pond. (He was quick to warn against the temptation to worship the pond, that is, materialism.)

Economic development from a Christian perspective consists, in part, of promoting that the right moral choice be made regardless of the financial consequences. But it must also be about improving the quality of choices our young people have before them. This is accomplished by developing businesses and creating entrepreneurial opportunities in order to give people the chance to own a piece of the pond.

The options in North Lawndale are scarce, to say the least. Economists tell us that the dollar turns over in North

SIGN OF HOPE

Lawndale once. In other words, dollars leave the community shortly after they arrive. We must go outside our community to buy groceries, shoes, appliances, toys, cars—and the list goes on. The "white flight" of the 1960s and 1970s included a mass exodus of businesses. Even most of those businesses still here in Lawndale are operated by people outside the community.

We have long recognized that such economic realities are not conducive to the kind of healthy, vibrant, growing community our church is seeking to build. Doing something about it has been perhaps the church's toughest challenge. Although there are many positive, inspiring stories associated with this ministry, most of the stories about our ventures in economic development, unfortunately, do not end happily but with lessons learned the hard way.

One of our earliest attempts at economic development was to start a construction business. The goal was to give young people marketable skills while turning a profit. But because these young men were still learning, they made mistakes. The mistakes meant the buildings cost far more to build than they should have, which in turn defeated one of our main ministry goals: providing affordable housing.

We opened a welding business with two goals in mind: training people to become welders and operating a viable, profit-making enterprise. We agreed in a handshake deal with a suburban businessman to repair garbage dumpsters. But after we had acquired about $75,000 worth of equipment, rented a building, and renovated a place out of which this business could operate, the suburban company began having financial problems. Eventually they informed us they had no work to send our way.

Since we had all the equipment anyway, we decided to go into the dumpster manufacturing business for ourselves, with the goal of providing dumpsters for Chicago restaurants. We actually signed a contract to make ten of them, but as things turned out, we were unable to deliver. Not only did we fail to meet the deadline but the ones we were able to produce were of an inferior quality. In short, we were not very good businesspeople. This business met its doom during an electrical blackout in Chicago, during which someone broke into our building and stole all of our welding equipment. As far as I was concerned, this was God's way of saying, "Do I have to hit you with a baseball bat, Coach? Close the welding business!"

Through these experiences, we learned an important lesson of economic development: it is almost impossible to accomplish job training and business development simultaneously. We would have been much better off limiting our purpose to one or the other. Our failures also taught me that trusting in God did not relieve us of the responsibility to develop necessary business skills and to apply good business sense.

On another occasion, we helped two women get off welfare, as they went to work manufacturing window shades for Perry Bigelow's suburban homes. Perry provided an example of a suburban-urban business partnership by looking to the city to find the labor to produce something his company needed. He set our workers up with everything they needed to have and know. But because Perry distributed the decision-making power at his company, his coworkers eventually decided to discontinue the window shades. And we could not find another market for them.

Although this business ultimately closed, it turned a substantial profit while it lasted, and those two women, armed with some work experience on their résumés, have not had to go back to receiving welfare. We learned, however, that a business venture must begin with sound market analysis.

Next on the list of noble efforts came dry cleaning. With this one we actually set a goal of making money for the ministry, which ended up being an unrealistic expectation. We did not have the equipment to do the cleaning on the premises. It was more of a drop-off business. People would bring their clothes here, and the business's sole employee would take them out to Reichardt Cleaners in the suburbs. (The owner, Bill Reichardt, serves on the board of the Lawndale Christian Development Corporation and is among our most generous and faithful supporters.) The business worked for a while, but then other nearby companies cut their costs to the point where we could not compete, given our expenses in getting the clothes to and from the suburbs. The business did, however, create one job for two years.

Not all the news on the economic development front in Lawndale, however, is less than sensational. By the time this book is in print, we will have opened a franchise of a restaurant chain that features what the *Chicago Sun-Times* considers the best deep-dish pizza in the city: Lou Malnati's. There are very few restaurants in our community to begin with, and not one of those is open in the evenings, except for takeout.

I met the Malnati brothers, Marc and Rick, about six years ago. They have run this Chicago-area franchise since their father's death in 1978. Reflecting our felt-need ministry philosophy, I told them that many people from the community had told me how great it would be to have a nice place where they could sit down and eat dinner and maybe even hang out for a while in the evenings. I explored with them the possibility of operating a pizza franchise, but we made no plans.

When in 1992 I heard that they were planning to open their ninth restaurant in the Chicago area, I challenged them to consider tithing a tenth restaurant for the purpose of

building the kingdom of God. I made a theological justifica-
tion for the request, explaining that the purpose of the tithe
(in Deuteronomy) was not for the good of the church per se
but to take care of the clergy and to care for the poor. I proposed that they tithe a restaurant to North Lawndale in order
to provide jobs and establish a place that symbolizes hope for
economic and community growth.

Marc and Rick were intrigued by the idea of tithing a
restaurant. We took a trip to New York City to meet with a
man named Joe Holland, who had started a Ben & Jerry's Ice
Cream franchise in Harlem. Joe, an African-American graduate of Harvard Law School, started the business to support
his ministry of providing housing for homeless men. Our trip
to New York helped convince us that a pizza place in
Lawndale could be economically viable.

It took us over three years, but I am confident that as you
read these words people are eating the best pizza in Chicago
right here in North Lawndale and that about twenty-five
men and women from the community have new jobs.
Families now have an alcohol-free place to spend some time
together. Young people have a safe place to hang out. Not
only did the Malnatis tithe a restaurant to North Lawndale
but they are also donating one hundred percent of the prof-
its to Lawndale Community Church. This money is ear-
marked to finance our efforts to expand our Samaritan
House program for the homeless, as well as our youth ministries and our College Opportunity program.

Our part in this deal was to buy and renovate the building that would house the restaurant and four Samaritan
House apartments above it. That was not hard to do, as word
of the generous example set by the Malnatis spread to our
supporters. One of our partners, Wayland Jensen, who owns
a window company, donated the front windows for the

restaurant and installed them for no charge. Another friend of the ministry, Dick Lauber, donated all the brick for the renovation, and several thousand dollars' worth of brickwork to boot. Even the city of Chicago, when they found out we were putting in a Lou Malnati's, put brand-new sidewalks around the whole restaurant, in apparent recognition of the significance of this step for our community. The building project has been coordinated by Drew Goldsmith, a twenty-three-year-old former marine who has been coming to church at Lawndale since he was ten. When the restaurant opens, he will continue working to ensure its success.

In addressing the bright side of economic development, I would be remiss not to mention the positive economic impact of Lawndale Community Church and its related ministries. People, no doubt, have various motives for supporting the work going on here. Government representatives have political motives. Some in the suburbs may support urban ministry out of a sense of self-preservation, recognizing that urban realities, whether positive or negative, eventually find their way out to the suburbs. But the overwhelming majority, I am convinced, support our efforts out of the purest of motives: service to humankind. In any event, there is clearly a "market demand," if you will, to bring health care, affordable housing, better education—in a word, hope—to this community.

We have a health center that is meeting the needs of the poor, but at the same time it is employing 100 people. Our church and a development corporation employ about 40 people. All told, the church and its ministries provide gainful employment for nearly 150 people, which represents a significant economic contribution to this community.

In addition to our business ventures, we coordinate various ministry activities designed to create jobs and enhance economic development. They take place under the auspices of our Imani program, the goal of which is to empower people, including the chronically unemployed, through teaching the skills they need to find jobs. "Imani" is a Swahili word that means "faith." The program purposes to develop faith in three areas. We want people to have *faith in God* and in his ability and desire to walk with them in good times and bad. We want them to have *faith in themselves* and in their talents and abilities to succeed. Finally, we want them to have *faith in the system,* confidence that there is room for them in the marketplace and that they can make it in America if they are willing to work hard.

In providing leadership for this program, Thomas Worthy meets with people individually and also teaches a class. Participants learn such fundamental skills as how to write a résumé and how to handle a job interview. Through Bible study, he explores the basis for having faith in all three of the dimensions cited above. We have been very successful at helping those who come through this program find jobs. Among other things, a budding demolition business has emerged from the Imani program. Thomas works with people regardless of their skills or current level of education. If they do not have a high school diploma, we channel them to a local Catholic church with which we have a working relationship in order to get them through a GED (high school equivalency diploma) program.

Our development corporation targets youth in two ways. We are in partnership with a New York City–based group called NFTE (National Foundation for Teaching Entrepreneurship). We put fifteen kids, ages fourteen to sixteen, through this program each year. During the twenty weeks of the program, they are required to own a piece of stock and start some kind of business. They get business cards, carry a briefcase, the works. All of it is designed to foster within them an entrepreneurial spirit.

We also have a program through which young people of high school age develop a positive work ethic and learn some kind of job skill in the process. They participate in the program for twenty weeks, during which time they might work at a construction site, or board up a few abandoned buildings, for minimum wage. They might learn how to use a screw gun, a hammer, and an electric saw. Others work in the health center as they explore career options in the medical field. In two hours of weekly class time, staff members talk with program participants about the meaning, the importance, and the essential goodness of work in God's design. We explore biblical principles that promote industry, using, for example, the story of Joseph and the famine in Egypt to promote a positive outlook on saving and planning for the future. Richard Townsell excels in these teaching situations, serving as an inspiration and superb role model for our young people. The leader who has been developed is now developing others.

All these programs and activities will serve our community well in the future, particularly if our young people choose to remain in Lawndale. We are not as far down the path of economic development as we would like to be. Perhaps we are not where we ought to be. But we are not where we used to be, either, and by God's grace, we are nowhere near where we are going to be just a few years from now.

Twelve

The Tools of Hope

IF PEOPLE PROVIDE THE source of hope for the future of our
community, then education provides the tools. It is virtually
axiomatic that education must play a central role in the pur-
suit of Christian Community Development. As children learn
to read, write, and do basic math their chances of contributing to our community and society increase immeasurably.

Unfortunately, a disproportionate percentage of those
who graduate from high school here in Lawndale have not
mastered these basic skills. On more than one occasion, the
Chicago school system has taken it on the chin. As mentioned earlier, William Bennett, during his tenure as U.S. education secretary, several times called the Chicago public
school system the worst in the nation.

Instead of hopping on the bandwagon, however, to criticize the three high schools and twenty-five public grammar
schools in North Lawndale, we at Lawndale have made a de-
liberate effort to support and augment the work of the
schools to every extent possible.

As someone who has worked in the Chicago public
school system, I know firsthand that many of its problems
are beyond the control of teachers and administrators.
Problems in schools more accurately reflect the general conditions of the inner city. As a school's negative reputation
grows the families and students who represent a positive

147

force typically abandon ship if possible, making things worse. By and large, teachers deserve our understanding and compassion, not harsh words of judgment.

We help our schools in several ways, including by having all the physicals for the sports teams given at the health center for a minimal charge. Ever since Secretary Bennett's less than flattering assessment, I have met with the four public grammar school principals in our target area on a yearly basis—just to find out how they are doing and if there's anything we can do to help.

At that first meeting, they said that anything we could do to encourage the teachers would be welcome, since morale was extremely low. As a result, for almost ten years running, the church has hosted all of these schools' faculty and staff for a yearly appreciation dinner in our gym. It is a catered event with a vibrant, celebratory spirit. We award plaques in such categories as the most creative or dedicated teacher. We regularly get at least eighty percent of the faculty and staff out for the event. Many of them treat it like their own version of the Academy Awards.

Each year, we also give every teacher and staff member at our four grammar schools a small gift as a token of our appreciation, and we give a gift of some kind to each school. Based on what they tell us they could use, we have contributed items ranging from computer software to microwave ovens to VCRs. We also give ribbons to students with perfect attendance.

Another way we support education and the mission of public schools in our community is through a tutoring program called Project LEAP (Lawndale Educational Advancement Program). It began as a traditional after-school tutoring program, with people from the church and volunteers from the suburbs working with children one-on-one.

PHYLON

Then the children began working with three or four computers that had been donated to the ministry along with some
software through which the children could develop math
and English skills.

In about 1988 we decided it was time to make a serious
effort to supplement the education of our public school system on a daily basis. We set up a first-class learning center
equipped with computers, books, and other educational resources. Today our learning center is home to about thirty
computers. Several on our education staff work with children
every day as part of our Umoja program. "Umoja" is yet another Swahili word and means "unity." The goal is to help
these young people develop into whole persons unified in
body, mind, and spirit. They play in the gym for a while after
school and then come to the learning center to do their home-
work or to work (and sometimes play) on the computers.
Our own teachers in the Umoja program teach skills in math
and in English. The children also have the opportunity to develop their creative abilities through activities such as story
writing and drawing.

In the summer we run what we call our Garden Program. The name is based on its goal of cultivating young
minds. We bring our own college students back for the summer and pay them to run the program. They put half their
money in the bank for college, give ten percent to further the
work of the kingdom, and spend the rest however they
want.

The Garden Program is a sort of combination vacation
Bible school, day camp, and summer school for kids of gram-
mar school age. They come from eleven in the morning till
about 4:00 in the afternoon every weekday for seven weeks.
We feed them lunches that have been provided by the city of
Chicago.

Melanie Casey and Precious Thomas oversee our educational programs. We teach these young people skills in five different areas. Three are related to their academic development: reading, math, and writing. We also work on skills related to their spiritual development.

The fifth area encompasses life skills. For the younger children, this might mean learning how to get help in an emergency or how to use public transportation. With the older children, we talk about sexuality, making sure to give the Christian perspective they might not be getting in public school or in the streets.

In addition to these skill areas, we teach these children African-American history, which is a focus I believe is lacking in public school textbooks and curricula. Whether they are black or white, we believe these young people ought to know about the great achievements that have been made by African-Americans in the history of our country. Our frequent use of Swahili words for program names is simply one more way to increase in all of us our appreciation of the African-American heritage. Many of these words have a richness that has no equivalent in Western languages.

Among our most important ministries in the area of education is the Lawndale College Opportunity Program, which we began in 1987. This is a five-year program in which students participate from the eighth grade all the way through high school.

The goal is to prepare young people to succeed in college. Three full-time staff members work with our College Opportunity Program, which is directed by Jenai Jenkins, an African-American alumna of Wheaton College. We pick a class of about fifteen people in the spring of their seventh-grade year. They begin the program the following fall. Twice a week they visit our learning center, where they learn to write papers. We have had Wheaton College professors come in to teach writing courses. We also prepare the students to take the SAT and ACT exams.

In addition to addressing their academic development, we help them prepare socially for college. They visit a college campus at least once a year. Every spring break and every summer, we take trips around the country to expand their horizons. With seventy-five young people involved with this program in any given year, we expect the number of college graduates living in Lawndale to skyrocket over the next decade.

Each year, we are able to secure between ten and twenty college scholarships for our college-bound youth through a partnership we have established with a group based in Glen Ellyn, Illinois, called Educational Assistance Limited. This organization works at getting businesses around the country to donate excess inventory, such as computer equipment and office furniture, to colleges, which in return provide scholarship assistance for those with financial needs.

Over the years, the competition to get into the College Opportunity Program has got heavier. Both Pastor Casey and I have spoken at assemblies in the schools, promoting all our programs, not just in our target area but throughout Lawndale. It is amazing the entrée we have in our school system as a result of our demonstrations of care and support.

Because we recognize the importance of parents in the quest to get into and through college, parental involvement is built into the application process. A parent must fill out one section of the application. Reference forms are to be completed by the student's primary teacher, the principal, and a church pastor or another adult. A parent must be present when staff and board members from our ministry interview candidates. Parents are also required to attend bimonthly meetings after their daughter or son is accepted into the program.

We continue to explore new ways to improve the quality of education in the community we seek to serve. Despite our support for the public school system, we have even considered starting an alternative high school. We are determined to do whatever we feel called to do and whatever is needed. We take the slogan of the United Negro College Fund very seriously: a mind truly is a terrible thing to waste.

Thirteen

Partners in Ministry

AT THIS POINT, I hope you are wondering, "How could I help an inner-city church like Lawndale?" The answer: become a partner, either individually or as a church. The story of the Lawndale Miracle cannot be told without mentioning the partnerships formed with churches and individuals.

My home church, First Baptist Church of Fort Dodge, Iowa, was the first to support us financially and by sending work groups that made the eight-hour trek to Chicago. Since then, churches at various locations around the country—though mostly in the Chicago area—have followed suit. Lawndale is a fixture on the missions budget of several churches. Of all the churches that have served us as partners, however, two stand out: Glen Ellyn Presbyterian Church and Christ Church of Oakbrook.

Glen Ellyn Presbyterian, through the efforts of close friends Pastor John Crosby and his wife, Laura, first got involved with our tutoring program fifteen years ago. Volunteers from the church came in to work with our children in the evenings. At about the time we were thinking of putting in a learning center, Glen Ellyn Presbyterian Church was approaching its sixtieth anniversary, but instead of celebrating by spending money on themselves, they decided to celebrate by supporting missions. They made a commitment of $45,000 to help us convert our "mini-gym" into a first-rate learning center for the children. Men and women from the church also made regular trips on Saturdays to help with the remodeling and to deliver supplies.

Back in 1981 Christ Church of Oakbrook also made a commitment to support inner-city ministry. They sent Ed Rose, the head of their missions committee, in for a visit. At that time we were a tiny storefront church with a few dozen people and a lot of dreams, but Christ Church of Oakbrook was able to envision the reality behind those dreams and began to support us financially on a monthly basis. As mentioned in Chapter 10, they gave us $60,000 in the first eighteen months of our housing ministry. It was crucial to getting us started. They also bought us a pickup truck about five years ago and a van before that.

The best suburban-urban church partnerships, however, consist of far more than an exchange of money and gifts-in-kind. They also include the development of meaningful personal relationships based on mutual trust and respect. Both suburban and city churches must make an intentional effort to go beyond the superficial. People from urban churches must take the time to educate their suburban partners with regard to their needs. Once a relationship of trust is established, people from the suburban churches must be willing to give up control in order to allow the urban church to continue on its path toward self-determination and self-sufficiency.

As I look back over the years of partnership with Glen Ellyn Presbyterian and Christ Church of Oakbrook it is these personal relationships that I value the most. Ed Rose is still the head of Christ Church's missions board today. He comes to Lawndale every few months to take some of the staff out to dinner. Early on in our partnership with Christ Church, some of their women came to Lawndale for a luncheon with some of ours. Then our women went out to Oakbrook. These

NORA

luncheons have continued through the years, leading to deep and lasting friendships. It warms my heart to know that our partnership with Christ Church consists partly of people calling and talking to each other on the phone and exchanging Christmas and birthday cards. While Christ Church has sent us several work crews, some of our people go to Oakbrook to participate in their annual missions festival.

Dr. Art DeKruyter, longtime pastor at Christ Church of Oakbrook, leads by example. I remember the day this highly respected, prestigious pastor put on his old blue jeans and borrowed an old pickup truck so he could deliver some large appliances to Lawndale. So what if the pickup was a stick shift that hopped up and down every time he tried to get it going, and then stalled out six or eight times.

His parishioners have followed his lead. Gene Eleveld for over ten years has served as volunteer accountant for our health center board, overseeing all its finances, which is a huge job. Radiologists from the church come in each week to read our X rays, which saves us thousands of dollars a year. Every once in a while, Don Kanak, who owns a computer store, brings us another computer. We now have thirty in our learning center, and we have never bought a single one. Don also provides computer consultation to make sure the systems run smoothly and efficiently.

Many people have partnered with us as individuals, based on the skills and abilities they have to offer. Several attorneys have done *pro bono* work in our behalf, including Brink Dickerson, who has donated his time to our church, and our development corporation, for nearly ten years.

Suburban churches typically have more construction workers, electricians, and artisans than they can use in a decade. Some of them have found their way to Lawndale. Dick Lauber, who owns a masonry business, built a six-thousand-square foot addition to our health center and church. I remember the day he showed me the blueprint for that addition and announced he was not going to charge us anything.

"That's wonderful," I told him. "Then all we have to worry about are the materials."

He corrected me. "No, we're taking care of all that too."

I said to him, "Dick, I didn't expect you to do that."

He replied, smiling, "No, and if you had, I wouldn't be doing it."

Dick has always made sure to give us absolute top-quality work. He is also known to come up with obscure Old Testament passages, such as the one about not bringing in wounded animals for sacrifice, to justify his insistence on quality. I would estimate that over the years, he and his workers have given us half a million dollars' worth of brickwork. With typical wisdom, Dick often brings different foremen in so they can see what we have going. He knows that many of them will be inspired and will end up donating their own time and effort. Sacrificial love is contagious!

In addition to Dick, Bruce Johnson has given us thousands of dollars' worth of architectural work. Alex Zera, a concrete contractor, has saved us thousands of dollars by donating his time and getting others to donate concrete. Sometimes Alex even pays for it himself.

In addressing the topic of partnerships, however, the first thing that comes to mind is parents. Almost to a person, the parents of those who have relocated in Lawndale have supported their children's call to ministry. My own parents, Lyle and Deleina Gordon, were also my first partners, providing not only material support but encouragement and advice, not to mention countless hours of prayer.

When I was sixteen years old, everybody told my mom and dad they were crazy for letting me move to the inner city for the summer. A few years later some folks told my parents I had wasted a lot of time and money earning a college degree just so I could live in the city.

When I graduated from college, my parents asked me what I wanted for a graduation present. I told them I would like a van so I could cart my kids around the city. I remember packing up all my possessions—my bed, my dresser, a desk, and all my clothes—into the back of that van when I moved to Lawndale. I lived out of it until I found an apartment. As planned, it became a regular source of transportation for the football team, wrestling team, and for kids from my Bible study.

The first workers to come to Lawndale to help out were my mother and father. After Anne and I bought our first building, they came immediately and spent almost two weeks with us, cleaning and painting.

Anne's mom and dad have also been faithful partners, despite their initial reservations about the life their daughter had chosen. I cannot count all the alarms my father-in-law put in our various apartment buildings and our medical clinic.

In thinking of moms and dads, the parents of both Art and Linda Jones also come to mind. After Art's dad (also named Art) retired as an accountant, he and Art's mother, Frances, began coming to Lawndale twice a week to do the bookkeeping for the health center. Linda's parents, Warren and Anneliese Lott, over the years have spent many a vacation here in Lawndale. After living in New Jersey most of their lives, Warren took an early retirement so they could move to Chicago and support their daughter's ministry. Now on our staff, Warren is one of those guys who can fix just about anything that's broken. Linda's mom comes in a couple of times a week as a volunteer to do office and clerical work.

I count my brother, Victor, as being among my most faithful ministry partners. Two years my senior, he is everything anyone could ever hope for in an older brother: an example of living for Christ. I have rarely made an important decision without consulting Victor, who now pastors a church in Wichita, Kansas. During my years as a part-time seminary student, Victor, the scholar in the family, coached me through more than a few theological mysteries (at least they were mysteries to me). Victor's church supports us both financially and by sending work crews.

Through the years I have also valued the partnership of friends, old and new. Kim Beisser, an old friend since high school days, was inspired by the dreams God had given me. After I moved into my first apartment, he hauled in a truckload of lumber, insulation, and paneling to fix up the apartment and the first weight room, which in many ways gave birth to the Lawndale Miracle. He even helped pay for the weight machine, and over the years, he has continued to donate tons of lumber and labor for our various building projects. Another friend, Ray Bakke, is also a mentor. He has spoken at the church, serves on our advisory board, and always seems to have access to whatever wisdom a situation demands.

Whereas a business partnership can be evaluated in terms of financial benefit, the value of friends as partners is both incalculable and invaluable. Among Anne's and my closest friends for over a decade have been Gordon and Cheryl Murphy. I cannot count the number of times they have sat with us, laughed and cried with us, offered guidance, and sometimes were simply there to listen.

Some people have encouraged and supported Anne and me simply by making sure we are taking care of ourselves spiritually and emotionally. Alex and Susie Zera and Dave and Karen Beré are examples of people who have looked out for our personal needs by taking us out to dinner, sponsoring "getaway weekends" for us, or getting together with us for fellowship.

In 1987 I was struggling with burnout to the point of being ready to give up. Anne and I shared our discouragement with Bill and Sabra Reichardt over lunch, and they decided that we needed a break. They gave us an all-expense-paid trip to Arizona for a week, with no agenda, no speaking engagements, and—perhaps most important—no kids! In just a few days' time, I was refreshed and ready to get back to work. Since then, Anne and I have made it a tradition to get away for a week each year just to be alone with each other and to deepen our walk with God.

There are people who look out for the well-being of others on the ministry staff as well. Bill and Nan Barnhart, for example, have made a financial commitment to see Stanley and Antoinette Ratliff's children through school, including college. These two couples get together regularly to see a play or go out to dinner.

Lawndale Community Church has also established meaningful relationships with partners who will never set foot in our community or even contribute financially but who are committed to praying for our ministry. We send out monthly prayer cards with a different request for each day of the month. We have over four thousand people around the world who pray for us regularly. We have lived the truth of 1 Corinthians 12, sometimes suffering and sometimes rejoicing as we have labored together for the good of the whole body.

Once when I was back at my home church in Iowa, an older woman took me aside, opened her Bible, and showed me my picture as it had appeared in the local newspaper back when I was in high school. She had had it laminated and used it as a bookmark as a reminder to pray every morning during her devotions for the people and ministries of Lawndale Community Church.

The benefits of partnerships, especially those between suburban and urban churches, flow in both directions. I'll never forget the phone call I received a few years ago from the youth pastor of a suburban church. He had just returned from a weekend retreat with about twenty youth from his own church and twenty from Lawndale. "Your kids, on average," he told me, "are two years ahead of our kids spiritually."

Frequently when work groups come down, they let us know that they are the ones who feel blessed. Bruce Johnson, Dick Lauber, and Alex Zera have all said the same thing. Dr. DeKruyter told me recently that I talk too much about how greatly we appreciate the people of Christ Church of Oakbrook. "You're the ones who have changed our lives," he said. "It is your people who have enriched the people of Christ Church of Oakbrook."

One partnership that has become increasingly important to individuals and ministries working among the urban and rural poor is the Christian Community Development Association (CCDA). At our 1994 gathering, 1500 people came to Baltimore from all over the country not just to share information and resources, but to support and encourage one another and to seek spiritual renewal. The board of directors spent the entire first day of the conference "bearing one another's burdens" in prayer. I remember going to one CCDA conference feeling discouraged and under tremendous stress. My brothers and sisters laid hands on me and prayed, and I wept uncontrollably as I felt my spiritual burden being lifted away.

Urban churches may also form a partnership with a ministry-minded publication, as many have done with the magazine *Urban Family.* I am recommending this magazine wherever I go as a resource to provide both hope and progress for urban ministries. In a time when the loudest messages we hear about the city are about decay, hopelessness, and problems that seem unsolvable, *Urban Family* tackles issues head on, offering genuine solutions based on strong moral values.

At first glance, it might seem strange that the people of our church and community have anything to offer those in the suburbs. But it begins to make sense to me when I consider what is truly important in life. I hope that the people of Lawndale will eventually be able to work at nice jobs, live in nice houses, and go to good schools. But in all honesty, I hope that life here never becomes exactly what it is in the suburbs today where amidst all the lush lawns, beautiful houses, and expensive cars can be found an epidemic of emptiness and loneliness.

Pastor Casey, not long before coming to Lawndale, attended a community Christmas party in his suburban Kansas City neighborhood. While at the party, he realized that even though he'd lived there for a number of years, he barely knew his neighbors. People from the suburbs typically drive to work and back in a car alone. When they get home they push the button on the automatic garage door opener and are safe inside before even making eye contact with another human being.

I've never been in favor of garages, or fences for that matter. Here in Lawndale our cars might be rusted, but we park them out in front of our houses. Our front yards won't win any awards, but they are places where people have friendly conversations and exchange smiles. I talk to people every day as I walk to and from work.

If I am out of town, Anne has a long list of people she can count on instantly if there is ever a problem. We are truly a community church. Not only do we worship together, but we work together and socialize together. We visit one another's houses, stop by to check on someone who is sick or depressed, deliver hot meals to those in need. The meal will still be hot when it gets there because it's only a block or two away.

What exists in Lawndale is a throwback to an earlier era in America when people had time for each other. Outsiders can sense when they come to visit us that we are all friends here. We know one another. We watch out for one another. We yell at each other's children when they get out of line. According to the African proverb, it takes a village to raise a child. Well in Lawndale, the entire church community is raising each of our children.

The sense of community here is not limited to people from the church. I was reminded of that in 1989 when someone took the three flags we have flying on the street corner closest to our church. We take a lot of pride in that beautiful street corner. The flags, along with the flowers and shrubs on the ground underneath, have become a hallmark of our community, a symbol of our future. I was fit to be tied when I discovered those flags were gone.

A few hours later, the head of the Vicelord gang came by and asked, "Coach, did you get the package?" ("Package" is often used as a code word for drugs, so I was a bit anxious to hear him say he'd left a package with my secretary.) After I told him I hadn't seen my secretary yet that day, he told me what was in the package: our flags. This gang leader had seen three guys running down the street with our flags draped around them, pretending to be Superman. He told me, "I pulled my car over and stopped. I got out and I said 'Give me back those flags. Don't you ever touch those flags again.

Those are the flags of Lawndale Community Church.'" No one has bothered our flags since.

Obviously, suburban living is safer, cleaner, and more comfortable than life in the inner city. But we in Lawndale experience daily a kind of community that is on the verge of extinction in suburban America.

The various parts of the body of Christ have much to offer one another. I strongly encourage urban and suburban churches all over this nation to reach out for each other and to explore the partnership possibilities. I hope that more and more suburban people will think about how they can use their businesses to help inner city communities. I hope they will view cities as sources of labor for the goods or services they produce. Many businesses in the suburbs hire urban workers who drive out from the city. I hope more will begin thinking about operating their businesses in communities of need and hiring people who can walk to work and remain fully a part of their community.

As thoroughly illustrated in this chapter, suburban churches and individuals can support urban ministries not only through financial contributions and no-interest loans, but by donating their skills, talents and energies. In reaching out in partnership, they will be enriched by the diversity of the kingdom of God. And if they look close, they will find people for whom faith is a reality and not a concept, people who don't have much money or possessions, but who have learned to trust God for what they need with a faith that is at once both simple and profound. They will encounter a sense of meaning and fulfillment for which many in the suburbs long, but that no amount of money can buy.

Part 4

The Soul
of the
Community

Fourteen

A Gospel for the City

I stand before you this morning because I have fallen short. I fell short by having sex out of marriage. I do not stand here because I think that I am any better than anyone else who has sinned, but for me to be totally free from this sin, I needed to voice what I have done openly because I have nothing to hide and am in no way ashamed. I do regret what I have done and know that it was wrong. I am, however, confident and secure in knowing that God has forgiven me. I ask that you would forgive me also.

I am a part of the Lawndale family. As a family, we are to work together for the betterment of every member. With this in mind, I ask today that you would help me with my spiritual development and in the raising of my beautiful son, Adon, who is nothing but a blessing from God.

God's word says: "I can do everything through him who gives me strength" (Philippians 4:13) and "God did not give us a spirit of timidity, but a spirit of power, of love and of self-discipline" (2 Timothy 1:7). With these verses in mind, I know that no matter what happens to me, I can and will be happy in the Lord. I hope my Lawndale family will do so, as well. Thank you.

—Markisha

When I moved to North Lawndale in 1975, my chief ministry goal was to lead others into a relationship with

Christ. One night I had the opportunity to do just that with one of my football players. I assured him that Jesus had forgiven him of all the sins he had ever committed in his life.

His response threw me for a loop. "Well, I don't think I've ever sinned before," he said. "I'm a pretty good kid."

I asked him if he had ever cheated on a test in school.

He said, "Yeah, I've cheated on tests. Everybody cheats on tests."

I asked if he had ever had sex with his girlfriend, and again he said, "Yeah, but everybody does that."

Before long I realized that "get saved" evangelism was designed for suburban folk. It had little meaning in an urban context. The needs of people in the city are not the same as those of people in the suburbs, where material and social needs are met and where people can be more easily motivated by feelings of guilt. People in the city are not encumbered primarily with feelings of guilt. Their deepest feelings are of hopelessness.

If the Christ of the suburbs is the Christ of forgiveness, the Christ of the city is the Christ of hope. Ultimately, of course, Jesus offers both, but recognizing differences in perceived needs plays an important role in forming strategies for evangelism.

Despite the many outreach ministries of Lawndale Community Church, none of them are more important than spending time with someone on a street corner, to pray, listen, or perhaps offer an encouraging word. Still, the church's efforts to provide quality health care, housing, and education communicate to the people of this community that we care about them. Such efforts would have little meaning in the suburbs, where housing, education, health care, and recreational opportunities abound.

ADON AND MARKISHA

Urban ministry has forced me to reconsider the role of the church—and my role as pastor—in a place where things do not always fall into place as neatly as we would like. I used to be extremely bothered, for example, by unmarried couples who were living together and yet came to church as if there were nothing wrong with their lifestyle. (These living arrangements are becoming more and more common throughout society, but they reached epidemic proportions in the city long ago.)

I began to realize, however, that God knew about these people who were living in sin and that he would deal with their behavior in his own way and in his own time. I realized further that their behavior was but a symptom of their not knowing Jesus Christ and trusting in the goodness of God's design for sexuality and for other areas of life. My job was to welcome all people who wanted to join us at church. After all, what is a church if it is not a place where sinners can come to learn about God's love, his forgiveness, and his will for our lives?

We teach clearly—from the pulpit and in all our programs—that sex is a wonderful gift from God but that God's plan calls for people to wait till they are married before engaging in sexual relations. We teach our young people that they will be blessed if they are patient and abide by God's plan and that they may face negative consequences in life otherwise. I have never diluted this message out of concern that someone in the congregation who is living in sin will feel judged or offended.

The role of the pastor in the city or anywhere else is to proclaim truth. Period. But challenging people with regard to their behavior, I believe, is the role of the Holy Spirit. At least a dozen couples over the years have come forward to say that God has challenged them regarding their behavior. They have claimed the forgiveness offered by Christ and moved on toward the goal of righteousness.

One reason I want all people to feel welcome at our church is based on the desire never to penalize children for being born outside marriage. I despise the term "illegitimate." In fact, I preach from the pulpit that there is no such thing as an illegitimate child. Instead what we have are promiscuous parents. We need to put our arms around those children and make sure they know they are accepted and loved. And we must not turn our back on the young woman or young man who is struggling with the consequences of mistakes of the past. We must help them to hear and personalize the message that Jesus makes all things new.

The statement at the beginning of this chapter was read in April of this year by a woman from our church who knows that past mistakes need not overcome future opportunities. Our congregation has committed to being a "father" for her child.

In light of our position opposing abortion, we seek to do all we can to meet the needs of unmarried women who are pregnant, seeing to it that they get proper prenatal care and are invited to join the life of the church. I am not aware of anyone who has left our church—or not come to our church—out of guilt for sins they have committed.

I have come to believe that many evangelicals wrongly regard some sins as being more heinous than others. "Suburban sins" of pride, materialism, racism, and systemic injustice—perhaps due in part to their subtlety—have in many quarters become more acceptable than such "urban sins" as substance abuse, petty crime, and sexual promiscuity.

Regardless of the nature of the sinful behavior in which people are engaged, we try to keep in mind the model established by Christ in the situation of the woman caught in adultery. There is a tension that exists between loving, forgiving, and accepting sinful people while at the same time challenging them to allow God's principles to govern all aspects of their lives. Most people have heard the admonition to "love the sinner but hate the sin" so many times they are tired of it. Saying it is easy. Doing it is hard—but necessary.

It is a very fine line we walk between offering the support people need in a difficult situation while rejecting the behavior that put them there in the first place. At different times through the years, I know we have erred at times by being too lenient and at other times by being too harsh. Leaders, including pastors, are imperfect and need forgiveness too.

Urban ministry has also meant having to be tolerant with people who are well meaning but who, because of the environment in which we live, sometimes end up in trouble. Today Anthony Franklin and I can chuckle about what we call the "radiator story," but it was no laughing matter eight years ago when the church van got impounded and Lawndale Community Church got a police record. I arrived at church at about six one Sunday morning and noticed the van was missing from its usual spot out in front of the church. Anthony, our night watchman at the time, had the keys, but he, like the van, was nowhere to be found. A few hours later as I was preparing for the 11:00 A.M. service, Anthony walked into my office and sat down. The first thing I noticed was the number written on his hand with magic marker, which I knew meant that he had been to jail overnight.

"Anthony, what happened?" I asked. He proceeded to explain that a couple of guys had come by during the night and asked if they could use the church van to move some radiators. Since he knew these guys, Anthony obliged and drove the van the two blocks or so to where the radiators were located.

DOUGLAS MOORE

Geraldine Moore, who helped start our church, is the mother of several sons. Leander, Andrew, and Walter played on my football team at Farragut. Walter went on to Taylor University, where he broke almost all the school's rushing records, and then returned to Lawndale to serve as youth pastor for three years. Unfortunately, his younger brother, Douglas, went in a different direction. In 1983, as a young man trying to find himself, Douglas got involved with some gangs in our community.

I was home eating lunch right after church one day when the phone rang. It was Leander. "We're all at the hospital," he told me. "Doug's been stabbed." I zipped the ten blocks to Mt. Sinai Hospital as fast as I could and found my friend Douglas lying on an emergency room table. It was the first time I had seen death quite so vividly.

One of my tensest days in ministry was the day of the funeral, which we held at our church amid rumblings that rival gangs might use it as an arena to continue their battles against one another. We called the police to put them on alert, and I stationed two of my bigger former football players at the door to inform people that we did not want any trouble. Over four hundred people crammed into our small building, in which there were only about a hundred chairs. Fortunately, our fears of further violence went unrealized.

For the service, the family had asked me to speak on the passage from the letter of James, which talks of life as a vapor and concludes that we do not know what tomorrow will bring. Indeed, there are so many things we do not know.

"Coach," one of Doug's brothers wanted to know, "is Doug in heaven?" I realized in that moment that Wayne Gordon does not hold the keys to heaven, nor does anyone.

"He is in God's hands," I told them. I believe we all can find some measure of comfort in that.

χ χ χ

As they were loading the radiators into the van a couple of police cars zoomed up to the spot. Everybody ran except Anthony, who was the only one who had no idea these radiators had been stolen and who was left holding the goods. They impounded the van and took Anthony off to jail. After fingerprinting him and making sure there were no warrants out for his arrest, they released him the next morning on "eye bond." Such is life in the big city.

Another daily reality of urban ministry is the tension that results from finding the right balance between compassion and discipline. Sometimes it is hard to know when we are helping people to help themselves and when we are merely enabling them to continue down a path that leads to destruction. When someone approaches us with a need, we try to meet that need in a way that goes beyond simply giving a handout. Carrie Moore, who has been a part of the church since 1978, heads our Benevolence Ministry. She talks with those who come to us with needs, in order to assess the situation and discuss various options.

People come to us on a daily basis with stories about how they need bus fare to go visit a sick mother or how they need a little extra money to buy groceries till the next check arrives. We never simply give money away. If someone needs money for a bus trip to Milwaukee, we will take that person to the bus station, buy a ticket, and watch him or her get on the bus. Carrie knows all the tricks of the trade, and she knows how to determine the difference between a legitimate need and a con orchestrated, perhaps, by someone trying to support a drug habit.

We strongly believe that charitable efforts must be of the kind that enhance human dignity and promote personal responsibility. Previous chapters have disclosed how we apply these values in the context of our health center, housing ministry, and various other programs.

I would be remiss not to address, before concluding this chapter, the perception that urban churches are virtually synonymous with needy churches. The people of Lawndale realize that at this point in our history, we have needs which we depend on outside support to meet. But we also realize we have a lot to offer.

I do not have to anticipate a time when we will be reaching out to other communities, because that day has already arrived. Lawndale Community Church is committed to contributing ten percent of what we receive in offerings to mission work outside our community. We support several African-American missionaries in other countries as well as in other parts of this country.

We support three physicians who started in our health center and have moved on to become missionary doctors overseas.

Several people have taken the ideas and the faith that were nurtured here and gone to other places of mission. We regard Andy and Debbie Krumsieg, for example, as Lawndale's ministry arm in St. Louis. We support them in their work with World Impact. As director, Andy attempts to take the principles through which God has worked in Lawndale to another city.

We have reached out to the Hispanic community in nearby "Little Village." In the mid-to-late-1980s the uninsured poor, most of them of Mexican ancestry, began to use the services of our health center, located just a few blocks north of Little Village. In 1989, at the founding meeting of the Christian Community Development Association, the Reverend Noel Castellanos approached me about his desire to do Christian community development in a Hispanic community. In 1990

Noel and Marianne Castellanos, along with their children, moved to Little Village, where Noel serves as pastor of LaViilita Community Church. We helped establish this church, which has enabled us to build bridges with the city's Hispanic community.

We have sought to demonstrate, through all these commitments, that the vision of Lawndale Community Church is far bigger than Lawndale. We are a community church, but one that has not lost sight of the fact that we are part of the worldwide body of Christ.

Fifteen

Giving Power Away

SOME SCHOLARS DEFINE THE whole of human history as a struggle for power. The effort to gain and hold on to power certainly characterizes much contemporary human activity, from Third World dictators to Fortune 500 executives. People spend years working and planning and waiting for power. Acquiring power is hard work. But one thing is harder: giving it away.

For some, "power" has bad connotations, even though power—whether political, social, or personal—can be used to accomplish both good and evil purposes. When we in Lawndale talk about empowering the people of our community, we have in mind the kind of power that will influence the world positively for the kingdom of God. We have in mind those people who, for various reasons, have not had access to the structures and decision-making processes that control their lives. Self-sufficiency and self-determination are virtual synonyms for empowerment.

During the 1980s I became more and more aware of how powerful a person I had become in Lawndale. Being a pastor of a church carries its own measure of power. Beyond that, our church—and its related ministries—had become a significant force in the community. My decisions and actions affected other people in greater and greater numbers.

My growing awareness of the things I controlled was accompanied by an increasing sense of discomfort with power.

In 1989 or so I read Tony Campolo's book *The Power Delusion,* which had a profound effect on me as I struggled with this whole idea of power. Campolo wrote about Christ's death on the cross, the fulcrum of history, as being in essence an act of giving away power. He argued that God works in the lives of people as they surrender their power in order to seek God's strength in the midst of their own weakness. He wrote that "powerlessness is a condition that frees a person to be prophetic."

These ideas made sense to me. I realized that people can indeed be more prophetic, free to speak the truth, when we have nothing to gain by what we say or do, when we are not worried about losing whatever position we have attained. Campolo used the illustration of many an aspiring politician who is incredibly creative and idealistic when trying to get elected. But after gaining access to that power, his whole thought process changes. He becomes less visionary and more pragmatic—because the goal is changed to simply hanging on to the power.

This same dynamic can occur in churches when a pastor gets more concerned with pleasing people than with speaking the truth. If we are not careful, we can end up being controlled by forces and ideas that are very different from those that motivated us in the beginning. No leader can be too careful in guarding against these potential negative effects of power.

In my personal devotions over the years, as I studied Scripture and prayed I found myself continually returning to this theme of giving away power. I began talking about it more, with Anne and a few others. Then, early in 1991, I read Henri Nouwen's *In the Name of Jesus,* a book of reflections on Christian leadership that crystallized my thinking on this topic. In it Nouwen focuses on the temptations of Christ, one

PASTOR CASEY

of which was the temptation to be powerful. At one point he writes, "One thing that's clear to me: the temptation of power is greatest when intimacy is a threat. Much Christian leadership is exercised by people who do not know how to develop healthy, intimate relationships and have opted for power and control instead. Many Christian empire-builders have been people unable to give and receive love." People cling to power, Nouwen suggests, to compensate for their inability to love others.

I became increasingly convinced that God was calling me to give away power. This, I realized, could be especially significant in view of the fact that I represented the majority culture in a predominantly African-American community. For the truth is that no matter how much I care about African-American people and identify with their past and present struggles, I can never know and understand life from their perspective. I will never experience what it is like to be a black person in America in quite the same way Eddie Jones has. Eddie was on his way to the health center one night to do some cleaning, when he was stopped by police and frisked. He happened to have several twenty-dollar bills in his pocket. An officer put a gun to his head and told him to get down on his knees as he and his partner handcuffed him.

They asked Eddie what he was doing with all that money. He explained that he worked as a janitor for Lawndale Christian Health Center and had just cashed his check. Upon finding the check stub in his pocket, the police let him go. "If you work down there with Coach Gordon," one of the officers said, "you must be okay." Eddie was justified based on his association with me—a white man.

On another occasion, two white interns from Wheaton College were sleeping in the church with E. J. (Elijah Johnson) and Anthony Franklin while our gym was being built. One of them, Dave Doig, later joined our staff for a while and is now deputy commissioner of housing for the city of Chicago. I remember on their first night in Lawndale telling Dave and the other intern to listen to Anthony and E. J. in the event of any problems, since Anthony and E. J. were streetwise.

At about two thirty in the morning, E. J. called to tell me to come over right away. Someone had driven a car into the church. I soon learned that two guys had been driving down Ogden Avenue shooting at each other. One got hit in the head and lost control of his vehicle. He later died at the hospital.

Fire engines, police cars, and an ambulance arrived on the scene. After things settled down, Art Jones asked the police if they could tow the car away, since we had church the next day. I instructed Anthony and E. J. to keep an eye on the car till the police arrived. Well, those two began to get curious, as did Dave and Jim, the other intern. The four of them thought they would do a little police work of their own and tried to get into the trunk to see if there were drugs in there. While they were at it they decided to help themselves to the car radio, since the car was totaled anyway. Then another person from the community happened by and laid claim to the tires.

About an hour after I had left the scene, I got another call, this time from Dave, who was having trouble composing himself. He told me the police had taken E. J. and Anthony to jail and instructed him to get inside the church, lock the door, and call me.

Should Anthony and E. J. have done what they did? No. Technically, they were stealing. But Jim and Dave did exactly the same thing. Their explanation that they were interns from Wheaton College—a story supported by the color of their skin—was enough to get them off the hook.

These are just two incidents that confirmed my view that regardless of my values or the commitments I have made to Lawndale, I do not have the right to speak for the African-American people here. If I am ever asked what the people of Lawndale think about something, I am careful to make it clear that I can speak only for myself.

I don't know when the day will come when people will not be judged instantly based on the color of their skin. I do know that it has not yet arrived. In pursuing that day, Jawanza Kunjufu recommends a three-step process for the development of relationships across cultures. First we must recognize the differences between us. Next, we must begin to understand those differences. Finally, we must move on to appreciate, celebrate, and even grow as a result of our differences.

Toward that end, I highly recommend that people read as many books by African-American authors as possible. One might begin with the books of Kunjufu, Richard Wright, John Perkins, Cornell West, Martin Luther King Jr., and Malcolm X.

Giving away power became an important part of my quest for racial reconciliation. Through the 1980s I took small steps in this direction by opening the pulpit to such African-American preachers and speakers as Tom Skinner, John Perkins, Dolphus Weary, and many others who are not household names. Among them was a dynamic young speaker and leader named Carey Casey.

In addition to feeling called by God to give away power, from a more practical standpoint I found that I was simply unable to do all that needed to be done to manage an eighty-five-member staff and oversee our church's outreach ministries while serving as pastor. I had trouble finding the time to visit people who were sick or to meet with those who needed help or guidance. Anne and I both realized that something had to give. Even though I still had a pastor's heart, we became increasingly convinced that the time had come for me to give up my role as senior pastor.

Many of my most trusted advisors within and outside Lawndale told me to take on an assistant pastor to help carry the load, instead of stepping down. But Anne and I felt certain that God wanted more than that. At a deacons meeting in May 1991, we disclosed what we felt I was being called to do: namely, to remain a part of the ministry but to step aside as the senior pastor of Lawndale Community Church.

For the first time since we had started the church, I was out of the equation. It was now up to the deacons and the congregation as a whole to determine where to go from here. Preaching the sermon the following Sunday was one of the hardest things I have ever done. I spoke about how God's power is made perfect in our weakness, citing examples from our own thirteen-year journey together. I recounted how time after time when it seemed to us there was no way to build a health center or a gym or to start some other kind of ministry, God provided the way. Then I explained that we were going to have to trust God once again.

I cried as I announced what I was planning to do, and most of the congregation cried with me. I almost could not finish the sermon. If there was ever any doubt, I realized then that walking in faith encompasses something more than following our feelings. What Anne and I were doing hurt. And yet we knew it was the right thing to do.

The next week, for the first time in the history of our church, the congregation began holding meetings without Anne and me present. Leaders began to emerge to define and guide the process. We received a small grant from World Vision to bring in an urban church consultant to help with the transition. What emerged was a plan to bring in a pastor who would neither be above me nor below me in authority but who would work alongside me as copastor. I would continue as outreach pastor; the new person would become the shepherding pastor and would assume the duties traditionally associated with pastoral ministry.

The church was committed to bringing in the best person it could find for this unique ministry position, no matter where that person might come from. The people drew up a list of criteria before starting the interviewing process. Some of the criteria were nonnegotiable: the new person would have to live in the community, have a heart for the poor, and care deeply about ministry to youth. Very interestingly, the congregation did not require that the new pastor be black, although that was both their preference and mine.

Prophetic as she sometimes is, Anne said, upon examining the criteria, "We need somebody like Carey Casey to come and do this." I had met Carey in 1984 through the Fellowship of Christian Athletes, of which he was the national urban director at that time. We put the word out around the country that we were looking for a shepherding pastor, and received a couple dozen résumés. Our deacon board, which handled the search, examined the résumés and began the interview process, eventually narrowing the field to two, one of whom was Carey. As one of the deacons, I participated in the process, my voice being equal with each of the others.

As it became clear that Carey was our first choice I decided to call him so we could talk. He and I, along with our wives, had been out to dinner a few times, and I sensed we were kindred spirits. But now that our relationship was on the brink of going deeper, I wanted us both to be sure we understood one another. I hopped on a plane to Kansas City and met him the next morning for breakfast.

Carey is fond of the expression, "Let's cut through the fluff and get to the stuff." That is exactly what we did that morning. I can still picture the scene at a Shoney's restaurant in Kansas City, where we sat for three and a half hours, asking each other point-blank if we could trust each other and imagining together what this copastor arrangement might look like. I wanted to talk structure; Carey wanted to know what we were going to do together.

After we left Shoney's, we were driving along and something popped into my mind that captured everything I wanted to say and learn that morning. "Carey, what I really need most of all," I said, "is a best friend, a partner in ministry."

It touched a responsive chord. Carey replied, "I can be that best friend for you." Somehow in that moment, on a street in downtown Kansas City, we both realized that this was right and that all the other details would fall into place.

In January 1992 the congregation voted to adjust the by-laws so that I could become outreach pastor and voted unanimously to install Carey Casey as shepherding pastor. He arrived in Lawndale in February. Just days before he arrived, I was reading a passage from 1 Samuel about the relationship between David and Jonathan and thinking about the friendship with Carey that was on the horizon. I read verse 4 of chapter 20, in which Jonathan tells David, "Whatever you want me to do, I'll do for you." I remember thinking how nice it would be to have someone like Carey to do whatever I wanted.

But the instant that thought entered my mind, I sensed the Lord standing beside me with a baseball bat ready to get a point across: "You got the right idea, bub, but you got it backward. That's what I want you to say to Carey." And so on Carey's first day here, we sat down together and prayed.

I told him about my experience in 1 Samuel and said to him, "As Jonathan said to David, 'Whatever you want me to do, I'll do for you.'"

A couple of days later I was in Carey's office and noticed he had his Bible open to that passage in 1 Samuel, which he had highlighted in yellow. Carey said, "Hold on a second. Go over there and read that verse, the one that says, 'Whatever you want me to do, I'll do.'" We both chuckled, but the point was made. I had to work at letting go. From the beginning, he had a way of reminding me of that without seeming harsh or getting upset.

I had to remember that for Carey, in some ways, this must have seemed like an impossible assignment. For one thing, he had come to a church where the founding pastor, who had also been the senior pastor for almost fourteen years, was still there. In an effort to make it easier for him, I gave him my office, which was not only bigger but was the kind of office the people had come to associate with the senior pastor.

Carey and I have had to work through several things together, as is the case with any friendship. But letting go became easier and easier as my trust and respect for Carey's judgments, intuition, and insights grew. Chief among those insights was his idea, early on, that the two of us meet for an hour each morning to develop our friendship and to make sure our hearts were right. I had been thinking more like once a week. As far as I was concerned, I was too busy to meet with anyone every day. But I submitted to him, and I am glad I did. Almost four years later we still get together each day at 8:00 A.M. sharp, and it is among the most important things we do. We support one another, pray together, talk about plans and goals and problems. We also hold each other accountable. The "fluff" left these meetings long ago.

We are able to confront and challenge one another openly and honestly. We have experienced together the truth of Proverbs 27, which states in essence that we grow from the wounds of a friend, not the kisses of an enemy.

Not only have we become close but our families have, as well. Every few months we get together for a potluck dinner at one house or the other. And contrary to popular perception, poor urban pastors are allowed to eat out every once in a while. Carey and his wife, Melanie, and Anne and I go out to dinner at least once a month—just the four of us—to talk and to pray. Sometimes we head out on a Sunday night to grab a cup of coffee together. The children have become friends as well. Patrice and Angela are the same age, as are Marcellus and Andrew. My son Austin, age seven, and Carey's daughter Christy, age seventeen, get along because, for some reason, they think it is neat to be ten years apart. It is easy for families to spend time together when they are separated only by four city blocks.

As shepherding pastor, Carey is in charge of preaching, pastoral visits, Sunday school, and Wednesday night prayer meetings. He oversees the whole Sunday morning worship service. I preach when he invites me to preach, which has ended up being once a month or so.

The toughest initial adjustment for me was not preaching every Sunday morning. I discovered the extent to which my relationship with God was tied up in preaching, since it was during sermon preparation that I conducted my in-depth Bible study, with the goal of coming up with fresh insights each week.

A few months after Carey's arrival, I asked him for and received permission to start a men's Bible-study group. I had been meeting with a group of about twelve men, called the Young Lions, every Wednesday for lunch. We gathered each week with no agenda except to talk. My ministry passion has always been to disciple black men and to teach the Bible. So we transformed the Young Lions into Kingdom Men. At first we met in the mornings, with five to ten men in attendance. To demonstrate our partnership, Carey came each week to sit under my teaching, as I came on Sunday mornings and Wednesday nights to learn from him. Kingdom Men has since moved to Monday evenings. About seventy-five men come for Bible study, after which we break up into small groups for prayer.

The friendship and working relationship Carey and I have built has been a model for our church and community. Nevertheless, although I have always been convinced that we have done exactly what God desired, sometimes the path has been difficult for me. In 1993, for example, the governor of Illinois came to Lawndale to recognize our health center and other ministries. One person was needed to be up on the platform with him, to serve as master of ceremonies and introduce him as speaker. I knew that person had to be Carey, even though I wanted it to be me.

I remember when the governor walked by me, shook my hand, and said hello. As far as he knew, I was just another face in the crowd. My selfish human nature was urging me to make sure I got credit for what we had accomplished, forgetting that all along I had given the credit to God and to the people. I was humbled. I had the same kinds of feelings the time Senator Paul Simon came to Lawndale and I had to be out of town. Carey was the one who got his picture taken with the senator and participated in the ceremonies of the day.

Carey, however, has displayed sensitivity in recognizing how important it is for all people, including Wayne Gordon, to feel affirmed. Not long ago Chicago mayor Richard Daley was here in Lawndale, and both Carey and I stood on the platform with him. I felt Carey's hand on my back gently pushing me, sliding me over between him and the mayor. When the pictures were taken, I was the one standing next to the mayor.

Another difficult experience for me came on the day Carey officiated his first wedding in Lawndale. It happened to be the wedding of Edward Daniels and Taneisha Green, both of whom I had known since they were snotty-nosed kids. It is always a special privilege for a pastor to bring together two people whom he has seen grow up together. But this time, Carey did the premarital counseling and performed the wedding, though I did have the chance to say a few words and offer prayer.

But even when the days are hard, I know they are right. I tell people that before the foundation of the world, God ordained Carey Casey and Wayne Gordon to be in ministry together. We like to joke that even our parents knew, while we were in the womb, that we would someday minister together. Carey's parents gave him the middle name Walden, which would one day make him feel more at home among white folks. My parents gave me the middle name LeRoy, a very common name here in North Lawndale.

Without a doubt, the opportunity to copastor Lawndale Community Church with such a man of integrity and vision as Carey Casey has been one of the greatest privileges of my life. He epitomizes the strength that lies in the African-American community, representing that community both locally and nationally with tremendous dignity.

My quest to give away power has not been limited to stepping down as senior pastor. I have also worked to give away power to Richard Townsell, who in 1992 took over for me as executive director of our development corporation. It has been a little harder with Richard, because I have known him since he was in high school. He was a part of our first leadership development program. It was Richard who coined the phrase "The Garden" for our summer education and ministry program for children. Over the years, Richard has written me unbelievably beautiful notes expressing his respect and his love for me. They are the kinds of things a son would say to his father in an ideal relationship. In fact, we have experienced some of the dynamics of a father-son relationship. Even though he is in his thirties now and ready to be out there on his own, I have had trouble letting go, because of my irrational fears that he will fail. As he rebels against the father image in me I become paternalistic and assume incorrectly that the only right way to do something is still, after all these years, my way.

Yes, we have struggled. But we have been honest with each other through those struggles. He has taught me many lessons as I walk down this sometimes lonely path of letting go. We have had some heated discussions. I have allowed him to make some mistakes that I would not have made. Other times when I have turned him loose to fail, things turned out more perfectly than I could have imagined or orchestrated on my own. Most importantly, we have been able to treat one another as equals—with mutual respect and love. I love Richard and thank God for all he has given and taught me.

I have also given away power to others who serve on the boards of our outreach ministries. For many years I was the president of all four boards and ran all the meetings. In October 1994 I resigned from the board of the health center, on which I had served as president for over eleven years. We are increasingly bringing our indigenous leadership on to these ministry boards. Donna Holt now serves on the board of the health center, along with Carey, Dave Doig, and Richard's wife, Stephanie. I now realize that as long I was there, too many eyes would look in my direction. Now new leadership is stepping to the fore. They are asking questions of their own about what to do next and how to do it.

I am confident that Lawndale Community Church will begin proving that it can not just survive but that it can thrive in my absence as I begin a sabbatical leave, which will begin about the time this book is released. My family and I will move out of Lawndale for a year. John Perkins and I will travel around the country to advise, encourage, and help build networks of support for churches and ministries in other cities. For the first time in eighteen years, I will be absent from the day-to-day operations of our church and ministries. The gradual process of letting go will, in some sense, be complete.

There were some tears when we made that announcement in church, even though our family is committed to coming back after the year is up. After all, Lawndale is our home. I don't know, however, what my new role will be when I return. Whatever it is, it can never be the same as before. The proverbial torch has already passed to the hands of others: people with strength, ability, and vision.

Giving away power—it has not been an easy thing to do. But it has always been the right thing to do.

Sixteen

Family Values

EPHESIANS 3:20 STATES THAT God is able to do "immeasurably more than all we ask or imagine." That verse first rang true to me when I met Anne Starkey. I fell in love with her right away, and it took a year to talk her into marrying me. For a long time I had thought about what my future wife would be like, assuming I got married. Anne exceeded even my greatest hopes and expectations.

After eighteen years of marriage, she remains my best friend. It is a friendship characterized both by compassion and candor. After a sermon she is my best critic. When I make mistakes, she is both unafraid enough to tell me and strong enough to support me. She has always expected me—and enabled me—to be a man of God, a loving husband, and a devoted father. I talk to her about everything, because I crave her insights and abilities.

I am aware that Anne had to give up many of her own dreams and aspirations, including a professional career. She graciously allowed my dream and the call of God on my life to become her own. She chose to stay at home as the primary caretaker of our three children: Angela, Andrew, and Austin. (Since I didn't get many A's in school, I decided to have a family of all A's!)

No one would ever guess that Anne never envisioned herself in a community such as Lawndale. God gave her the gift of friendship, a gift she has shared not just with me but with this entire community. If friendship is an art, Anne is a virtuoso.

Shortly after we had moved to Lawndale, an incident took place that illustrates Anne's powerful gift. She was sitting on the steps below our Ogden Avenue apartment, with the eight-year-old girl who lived next door. This child shared her heart with Anne about how her teacher at school had not been very nice to her. She blurted out, "My teacher's white." Tragically, the child had learned at that young age to associate mean people with white people.

Anne said to her, "Well, I'm white too."

The girl replied, "You're not white, Miss Anne. You're just light."

Anne's love was such that this child claimed Anne as one of her own.

The people from our church cannot fathom how Anne is able to be so close to so many. She develops her friendships over coffee, over lunch, and over the phone. Anne and I can interact with the same person on the same day in the same setting, but unlike me, she can tell when someone is hurting or struggling with a problem.

About ten years ago a passage from Ephesians 5 hit me right between the eyes. God was telling me to love Anne as Christ loves the church. Christ, of course, died for the church. I realized that I was being called to love Anne the same way, even if it meant my dreams in ministry would not survive. I was being called to love and care for her as I would for my own body. As an athlete, I was aware of the commitment required to take care of the body. Since that time, I have tried to focus my attention on loving my wife, though many times I have fallen short.

Having children, of course, totally changed our lives, as it does for all people. Even some who totally understood my

ANNE AND COACH

call to live in the city wondered how I could possibly raise a family in an environment saturated with drugs, violence, and substandard schools. Most people have too much trouble seeing past the "downside" of urban living to appreciate its many benefits.

All three of our children were born in Lawndale, and each has experienced life here in different ways. I will never forget how the first, Angela, perceived racial differences as a youngster. (Anne and I had decided early on not to talk about black people or white people but only about people. We describe people in terms other than the color of their skin.) Angela traveled by bus to an elementary school about ten minutes away. One night after kindergarten, she told us at dinner that she had been slapped on the bus for no reason. The girl who had slapped her, she said, was "black like me."

Anne and I decided to forego clarifying this minor technicality regarding her racial identity. But not long after that, I was at her school for an assembly and decided to ride home on the bus with Angela so she could point out to me this girl who was "black like her." We saw several cute little African-American girls in pigtails hopping and bopping onto the bus, but Angela didn't say anything. Then a few white girls got on, but still she was silent. Finally she started poking me in the ribs and saying, "There she is." Onto the bus walked a little girl who was neither black nor white. She was a Hispanic girl from the Mexican community, whose skin color was very much like that of my daughter, who is dark complected.

I realized that Angela, at age five, perceived that all people were black. Some black people were different from her, while others were black just like her. But ultimately everyone was the same. We merely came in different shades. I remember thinking back then how much God must desire all human beings to view one another as part of the same human race, replete with various shades of color. Outside Lawndale Angela and I would have been deprived of this lesson.

As things turned out, that story defined Angela's personality. She very naturally loves everyone, gets along with people of all races: Puerto Rican, African-American, white, Italian, and others. If an ethnic group is present in Lawndale, my daughter not only knows but likes someone who hails from it.

My third child, Austin, also taught us a very important lesson as a youngster. Angela, who was doing a report for school on Martin Luther King Jr., had brought several books home. In paging through one of them, Austin found a picture of the Ku Klux Klan in action: stick-bearing figures on horses, with sheets draped over their heads. A bit frightened, Austin asked his mother who these scary-looking creatures were.

Anne explained in four-year-old language that they were men who did not like black people and did mean things to them. Without missing a beat, Austin said, "Then Daddy and Angela better look out." Because my skin and Angela's skin was darker than Austin's and his brother's and mother's skin, in his mind Angela and I were black. That night, Austin taught me that being a member of a family is not based on our skin color but on the relationship we have. We would not have learned that lesson outside of a place like Lawndale.

When my older son, Andrew, was eight, he got some money for his birthday. He had been hoarding money for quite a while—to the point where he had saved a whopping sixty-eight dollars. We encouraged him to think of some ways he might spend some of that money, and he thought about it for several weeks. One Saturday night, we got home late from a program at church. I had just got the kids to bed when, at about ten o'clock, the phone rang. Someone had showed up at the church, needing twenty dollars to fix a car that had broken down.

We generally do not give somebody twenty dollars without checking into their story. I told this man over the phone that we would give him a ride home and help him get his car fixed on Monday. But all he wanted was twenty dollars, so I finally had to tell him I did not have twenty dollars to give him. Again I offered to give him a ride, but he declined. As I hung up the phone I turned around to find Andrew in his pajamas. Having sensed the drift of the phone conversation, he handed me a twenty-dollar bill. "Dad," he said, "I want to help that man get his car fixed." I assured my son that if the man came back Monday, I'd use his twenty dollars to help fix the car. The man did not return.

A few weeks later Andrew had another idea. We had been having some break-ins in the church parking lot during a time when we were trying to get a women's Bible study started. The women were afraid to come out at night because of these break-ins. The lot was dark because all the streetlights nearby had been broken. The church had been talking about putting in some lights of our own, and apparently Andrew had overheard some of these conversations as well. After I walked in from work one day, he stood there, holding a Service Merchandise catalog opened up to the lighting section. He had his eye on some lights that cost $39.95, and he wanted to buy them for the church parking lot so the women could come to Bible study. It was hard for me to tell the little guy that these were the kind of lights that people out in the suburbs put along their sidewalks. Nevertheless, Andrew's unselfish willingness to give assured me that my children were learning the kinds of values I wanted them to learn.

Of course, living in the city has some drawbacks. We try to be very careful about knowing where our children are at all times. If we allow them to walk the streets alone, we make sure someone calls when they arrive safely. As they get older they are beginning to think we are a little too protective, especially since some parents in the community are more lenient.

─────── *LET JUSTICE ROLL DOWN:* ───────
THE STORY OF JOHN PERKINS

A book report by Andrew Gordon, age 11.

The first half of his life: John Perkins lived on a big farm with his family and other blacks that was owned by a white man and his family. They got paid very little money. So his aunt had to run a moonshine business.

I think that Clyde was his favorite brother because he was one of the only blacks that stood up to whites at that time. I think because of that reason he got killed by white officers.

His father was never around and he only got to see him once or twice in his life.

Later in his life: He got sent to California and while he was in California he got married and got a good job. While he was in California he met the Lord. In California a few years later he felt God was calling him back to Mississippi but he did not want to go because he was doing well in California and he did not want to move back to a place of hatred.

He prayed and God told him to go back so he did, but it was hard. When he moved back, he got a church together. While he was trying to make it better for the blacks of Mississippi, he got beat many times and got called names many times. But I believe we should try to make it better for every human being in this world just like John Perkins did. That's why I call him Grandpa Perkins.

────────── ✗ ✗ ✗ ──────────

We take these precautions even though we have never had a problem. People who have lived in cities realize that the dangers are overrated, due in part to the cumulative effect of the media's coverage of violence. I would never try to convince anyone that the inner city is as safe as the suburbs. But neither is it a war zone. People who hang out in the wrong places and do the wrong things expose themselves to danger. But those who are not seeking trouble generally will not find it.

We have been able to create safe havens for the children of Lawndale. Our backyard is a place where neighborhood kids can come and play. We have a little swingset, a small homemade fort, and a raggedy old basketball hoop about seven feet high. That's enough, in the eyes of the kids next door, to refer to our backyard as "the park."

The church and our gym have also become safe centers of positive activity for community children, many of whom participate in our education programs or just come to the gym to play basketball. Like many African-American youth, Andrew would play basketball all day if I let him. He has been accepted in this community and feels very much at home within the African-American culture. (He is even turning into a pretty good basketball player—if I do say so myself.) Andrew has also had regular contact with white suburban culture, mainly through our trips to visit relatives and friends. I consider him genuinely bicultural, a trait I am sure will serve him well in the future.

One of the things Anne and I have struggled with is our children's schooling. From the beginning, we have supported the public school system in our community, despite its shortcomings, and have remained committed to sending our children to public school—at least through elementary school. We realize they probably will not receive as good an academic education as they might elsewhere. But through living in the city, they are learning about life and other cultures in ways that simply would not be possible in a more homogenous community. They see from up close, for example, the ravaging physical and emotional effects drugs and alcohol can have on a human being, and so are not persuaded by the glamorized portrayals of the "good life" so prominent in the media. If my goal as a parent was to make sure my children would never abuse drugs or alcohol, the best thing I could have done was to bring them here to grow up.

We continue to supplement our children's educational experience through church programs and at home. And we have attempted, on a case-by-case basis, to find the right balance between our support for public education and our desire for our children to have a good educational experience. This resulted in our recent, difficult decision to send Angela to Timothy Christian High School in suburban Elmhurst.

The quality of public education, despite the efforts of many capable and dedicated teachers, drops off severely from elementary school to high school. People from the church have understood that Anne and I, like any parents, want to do what is best for our children. The fact that Angela is not the only one from our church to attend private school—nor was she the first—makes it easier to feel comfortable about it. In all, seven students from Lawndale attend Timothy Christian, including Pastor Casey's daughter Patrice, who is one of Angela's closest friends. Since the fifty-five youth of high school age in our church attend a total of more than twenty-five different high schools, those who go out to Timothy Christian are by no means conspicuously absent from other local schools. The school sends a bus to Lawndale to pick up our kids and return them in the afternoon, making it very convenient for our young people to attend.

City living, for our family, has included the joy of sharing an apartment building for the last fifteen years with the Art and Linda Jones family. Their children—Kelly and Katelin—are like cousins to Angela, Andrew, and Austin.

But we still live in the city. People ask me all the time if I wonder how my children are going to turn out for having lived here. They wonder aloud if Anne and I are sacrificing them at the altar of our commitment to ministry in Lawndale. It almost sounds as if people think it is torture for our children to have to live here, when in fact nothing could be further from the truth. Lawndale is their home. It is a place where they have found friends and experienced community. It is a place they love. When I announced that we would be leaving Lawndale for a year so I could go on sabbatical, they did not cheer. Instead they were disappointed, because they don't want to leave.

From my perspective, I have trouble imagining anyone thinking we have somehow handicapped our children's futures by bringing them up in Lawndale. They are learning kingdom values here that I am not sure they could have learned anywhere else. Their world is a microcosm of the real world. Whereas other children learn about diversity, our children experience it daily, to the point where accepting and appreciating other cultures and ethnic groups is second nature.

Do I wish our streets were safe enough that I never had to worry about my children walking them? Certainly. Do I wish our schools could offer young people a better education? Definitely. Do I have any regrets about raising a family in Lawndale? Absolutely not.

Seventeen

Living the Miracle

AS YOU HAVE SEEN, the story of the Lawndale Miracle and the real hope it has offered to Chicago actually consists of many smaller stories: stories about people who, by God's grace, have overcome the odds against them and are poised to lead Lawndale into a brighter future; stories about churches and individuals who lost touch with the typical suburban values of materialism and greed in order to be a part of something truly important; stories about a community pulling together to accomplish goals and to fulfill dreams that many thought impossible.

I have saved the story of the William and Vanessa Little family for last, because in their story can be found all the essential elements of the Lawndale experience: violence, tragedy, struggle, faith, commitment, perseverance, hope, growth, and abiding love.

For a long time the Littles have been among our closest friends in Lawndale. Vanessa's brother, Dwayne, played on my football team at Farragut. I met Vanessa as a result of a tragedy in her family. Anne and I walked with them through their time of crisis, trying to offer counsel and support. Vanessa began coming to church. One Sunday she made a commitment to follow Christ. It revolutionized her life; she has been living for Jesus ever since.

William and Vanessa have made themselves available through the years to anyone in the church who has a problem.

Vanessa has served the church in many different ways. For a time she was the head of our furniture and clothing thrift store and food center. She now serves on the staff of the health center. Among her responsibilities is overseeing our program, operated out of the Public Aid office and designed to cut through the red tape of bureaucracy in order to assure that pregnant women get the medical care they need. Vanessa is also one of the deacons of the church and the organizer of Kingdom Women, a Bible study group that meets on Saturday mornings. People who see Vanessa at work are amazed to discover that she never went to college. She has not allowed that to keep her from rising to the position of leadership God has carved out for her.

It did not take long after Vanessa started coming to church for her and Anne to become friends. Over the years, they have got about as close as two friends could possibly be. They talk on the phone every day and do things together almost every day. This is what happens when two people with the gift of friendship find one another. Theirs, however, is not a selfish friendship. Both Vanessa and Anne can spot needs from an incredible distance, and it seems they always know exactly what word to say or supportive action to take.

In 1979 Vanessa and William's firstborn, William Jr., was nine years old. The church quickly became his second home, sometimes even his first. He went on to play football at Farragut, just like his uncle Dwayne. I coached "Little William" by giving him some pointers on the side, as this was after I had left Farragut. He attended Bible studies, church, and Sunday school faithfully all the way through high school.

We quit calling him "Little William" when we realized he was bigger than his daddy. He had matured in other ways as well. Eventually he went off to study at Western Illinois

THE LITTLE FAMILY

University. I remember taking his younger brother, Jason, and my son Andrew with me to visit him there. During his first two summer breaks, William worked at the church, doing whatever needed to be done. The summer before his senior year, he expressed the desire to become part of our Leadership Development Program.

One of the required readings that year was *The Autobiography of Malcolm X*. At the time, the movie was getting a lot of prerelease publicity, and I wanted the young people to find out for themselves who this man really was. William read this book in addition to working with the children in our Garden Program. As the end of the summer drew near, he came to me and said, "Coach, when I graduate, I wouldn't mind coming back and working in the ministry." William Little sure knew how to make my day.

When he graduated in 1993, we had a job waiting for him in our housing ministry, at a time when we had just begun thinking about a $3.5 million apartment renovation project. William paid his dues, spending the first year doing mostly grunt work as he learned the ropes. He later went on to serve as coordinator for the Lazarus Project, overseeing the renovation of forty-eight apartments in our community. At age twenty-five, William Little has experienced empowerment. He is a Kingdom Man; he comes to church weekly and is also involved as a volunteer with our youth ministry. He is the kind of person any father would be proud to claim as a son.

I have known William's younger brother, Kenny, literally since he was in diapers. Kenny was barely a month old when his mother brought him to church in 1979. Back in those early days when we had just forty or so attending, Kenny and my daughter, Angela, were often the only two kids in the nursery. Those two grew up having all kinds of fun together at church.

After Kenny learned to crawl, his mom and dad would turn him loose in my office, where about five or six of us met each week for a Sunday school class. Kenny would take every book he could reach off my shelves and distribute them around the room. It used to take us fifteen minutes to put the place back together. As things would turn out, however, Kenny's fascination with books and with learning stayed with him. I believe the Lord has big plans for Kenny Little. He is now sixteen, is in our College Opportunity Program, and has been in tune with Christ from the time he was a little boy.

After William went off to college, Kenny became our "sound man" at church when he was only ten. He still holds that position today. Dependable to a fault, Kenny is in charge of all our sound equipment. He runs the tape machine to record the sermons, sets up the microphones and loudspeaker system, and is not satisfied until the sound is as good as it can possibly be. Over the last six years whenever Kenny has been sick or out of town, the whole church can tell he is gone—simply by listening.

Through the years, Kenny has stopped by my office many times. Since he was eight or nine years old, we have been able to talk together, friend to friend. We have always had a special relationship. I am so glad I was able to be there for him in December 1994, when just before Christmas he lost one of his closest friends in a house fire. This young woman had been active in our youth group and attended school with Kenny. Sensitive young man that he is, this tragedy hurt him to the core. His mother called to say Kenny needed to talk. At the funeral I let him cry as I held him in my arms, as a father holds a son. Together we have pushed on through this tragedy. I am as proud of Kenny Little as I am of anyone I've ever met.

E. J.

In 1981, a woman from the community brought Elijah Johnson, "E. J.," to our door. She had encountered him at the local grocery store. He had asked if he could carry her bags to the car for a quarter. Homeless at age sixteen, E. J. had fled an abusive situation. When we met him, he was staying in an abandoned apartment building with no heat and sleeping in a bathtub there. He did whatever work he could to feed himself. Amazingly, with no one to prod him, he made sure he got to Farragut High School every day.

Though he was a hard worker, E. J. struggled in school. Because of a speech impediment, people sometimes misunderstood him or made fun of him. He soon became a sort of child of the church. He ate dinner regularly with four or five different church families and afterward would take a shower. We renovated a little space for him in the old Cadillac building that we were turning into a medical clinic. He and Anthony Franklin became the night watchmen. They had little loft apartments upstairs, where they stayed even after we opened the medical clinic.

Since E. J. had no place to spend Christmas one year, he came over to our place on Christmas Eve and stayed the night. He had no previous memory of waking up on Christmas morning with gifts under the tree for him. That year was different. We spent the day together as a family, and it was one of Anne's and my most memorable Christmases.

As we anticipated E. J. graduating from high school I knew it might be hard for him to get a job, but I also knew that once an employer hired him, the employer would find it hard to let him go. So I approached a local businessman who had no budget to hire anyone. I offered to give him forty dollars a week to give to E. J. for working after school for a few hours three days a week.

Before long this businessman told me E. J. would now be working every day after school. He said, "You don't have to give me any more money. I'm getting a lot out of E. J. He's a hard worker." After E. J. graduated from high school, he went to work with this business full time.

I've kept a folder with E. J.'s things in it, such as his high school report cards and the letter from school the time he got suspended. The folder includes cards he got me on Valentine's Day two years in a row. One year the card said, "Dad, all the wonderful things you are add up to one wonderful guy. Happy Valentine's Day." And then, in his own writing, E. J. added, "To Coach, as a dad, I just want to say thank you for everything you did for me. Love always, E. J."

E. J. is not here with us anymore. A family from our church knew someone in Arkansas, and he decided to go there to work in a cotton factory. E. J. calls me every few months. As of this writing, things are not going as well as we'd hoped they would. While living in Lawndale E. J. became a Christian, but he's now struggling with his faith. And a cotton machine cut off three of his fingers.

Many of the stories of the people of Lawndale are still "in process." E. J.'s is among them. I hope and believe he'll return one day. We miss him here immensely.

——————————— ✗ ✗ ✗ ———————————

And then there is Kenny's younger brother, Jason. Vanessa was pregnant with Jason during the same time Anne was carrying Andrew. In fact, they were due on the same day. It seems these two children were destined from the womb to follow the example of their mothers by becoming the closest of friends.

That is exactly what has happened, even though Jason arrived a week early and Andrew came along two weeks late. For as far back as those two can remember, they have been accompanying their mothers to the grocery store or to lunch. Today, as sixth-graders, they play basketball together and do other things together. To say they are best friends is an understatement. Those two guys are virtually inseparable. Jason sleeps over at our house, and Andrew at the Littles. In fact, my son is over there so often, they call him Andrew Little. He and Jason are like brothers. Both are a part of our More Than Conquerors youth ministry, which is led by youth pastor Phil Jackson. They meet on Sunday nights for various activities, including in-depth Bible study.

Meanwhile the father of the Little household, William, is exactly the kind of person for whom our Rehab for Ownership housing program was tailor-made. He is a hard worker who is totally committed to providing and caring for his family. When his suburban employer a few years back closed the plant where William had been working, they found him another job with the company, because of his work ethic.

The Littles were among the first church families to move to South Avers Street, one of the most dangerous places in the city. Ironically, when we first started talking about buying property on South Avers, Vanessa said I must be off my rocker. But not only was William open to the idea, he was even a little excited. He persuaded Vanessa to go over one day just to take a look at the house we were thinking about buying.

We went over to the house together and prayed about what the Littles should do. Of course, the house was a wreck: broken windows, chipped paint, the works. As Vanessa was asking God if he really wanted them to have this house, she looked out into the backyard. There amid the broken glass and scattered trash, she saw a flower, a daisy that had somehow managed to find life there among the weeds. She quickly came to interpret this daisy as a sign of hope from God. She began to think that this house could become a flower, a sign of hope for the community, a foretaste of its future.

The Littles joined the Rehab for Ownership program, and the things William did with that house were absolutely stunning. He built walls and steps, put in floors, hung all the drywall. He went way over and above the call of duty. We expect a couple hundred hours of sweat equity; I'm sure William put in at least a thousand hours. I have never seen a man work so hard for so long on a house. The efforts paid off. William and Vanessa succeeded in turning this eyesore into a flower of hope for their new neighborhood. The Littles moved into it in 1989.

As part of the program, we hold a service of celebration when someone goes to their newly refurbished residence. Part of the purpose is to make sure the people realize that their house is no longer just a house but a home of which Jesus Christ desires to be at the center. Knowing how hard the Littles had worked and how important this house was to our goal of reclaiming this neighborhood, this dedication was especially meaningful.

In accordance with our tradition, we go to each newly renovated house right after church, bringing along four gifts for the family. The first is a loaf of bread, representing both Jesus as the bread of life and our faith that the family would never go hungry. The second gift is salt. This symbolizes both Jesus Christ as the salt of the world and their new home as salt for the neighborhood. We also talk about salt as representing God's faithfulness in providing a Christian flavor to their family.

Thirdly, we give a gift of light, usually in the form of a flashlight. Not only will this help them find the circuit breakers if the electricity goes off but it also represents the hope that they will become a shining light in their neighborhood, a light through which others will be drawn to the light of Jesus Christ. Finally, the families receive a nice, leatherbound Bible, presented with the prayer that God's Word would remain at the center of all they do.

I can still remember giving William his Bible. When I see him carrying it in church, I am reminded of how hard he worked for it. He continues to work hard. That house is immaculate inside and out. Many flowers now decorate the yard where there was once just a solitary daisy. And I would defy anyone to find even a single weed. No sir! Not in William Little's yard.

The Littles are among our closest and most long-standing friends in Lawndale. A few years ago they gave us a little plaque that hangs above our kitchen sink, with the words, "Best friends are a gift from God." We're over at each other's houses week in and week out, whether for birthdays, graduations, other celebrations, or just to talk or watch a game on TV. Among our traditions is getting together each year for Good Friday dinner.

Through the years, the Littles have been a consistent source of moral support. When I stepped aside as the pastor, Vanessa was one of the first to write me a note of encouragement. When I announced that I would be going on sabbatical, she knew how hard it was for me and wrote another note that said, "Coach, I love you. Trust the Lord. Everything's gonna be okay." In an age when many children are being raised by a single parent, my children have more than two. If Andrew is struggling with a problem, he knows he can talk to Vanessa, a counselor as well as a friend. Andrew has experienced her long track record of giving good advice.

The Littles' experience in Lawndale, however, has been touched by tragedy, as is the case with many people. In 1986 one of Vanessa's sisters was murdered, stabbed to death. She left behind two daughters, Lakeisha and Nicole. They moved in with Vanessa's mother until she died about four years ago, prompting William and Vanessa to begin praying about what they should do.

The Littles ended up proving that love and commitment are thicker than blood. William and Vanessa became legal guardians for "Keisha" and "Niki," as we call them. For the last four years, the Littles have raised those girls like their own daughters. A newcomer to Lawndale would never know that Keisha and Niki were not part of the Little family all along. Keisha graduated from high school in 1995 and remains a part of our College Opportunity program, through which she is receiving scholarship aid to attend college. Niki, now in junior high school, will probably follow in her sister's footsteps.

In sum, the Little family, more than any other, represents the full range of what people, especially those who have participated in the Lawndale Miracle, have experienced in this community over the last twenty years. My account represents only a small fraction of that experience. There are other people to acknowledge and many more stories to tell. I can only hope that you have been able to capture a glimpse of the excitement, of the constant air of expectation that runs throughout the story of the Lawndale Miracle as people of humble, persistent faith reach out to offer real hope to Chicago.

What we call the Lawndale Miracle ultimately revolves around a worshiping and praying community of believers. Together we have witnessed and experienced the power of the Lord at work transforming individual lives and a community's spirit. The Sunday morning worship service—a time of uninhibited praise, prayer, preaching, and sharing—provides the spiritual focus and strength that undergirds all of our outreach ministries. For me personally, many times through the years God has provided through the people of the church just the right insight or word of support to lift me from my depression or discouragement. Sometimes it comes after the service in the form of an unexpected phone call or note.

The Lawndale staff, the overwhelming majority of whom are persons of color who live in the neighborhood, reflect this same love and support of the body of Christ. To work for Lawndale is more than a job. It is a ministry. I am humbled by the quality and commitment of our 150 or so paid staff. It is amazing to me the team of people God has assembled in Lawndale. One way we remind ourselves of our ministry is by getting together as a staff each morning to sing and pray and twice a month for an extended time with no agenda except to share personal and ministry struggles around God's Word and to uplift one another in prayer.

I consider myself the most privileged person on the face of the earth, to have had the chance to be a part of the Lawndale Miracle. I feel honored to have had the opportunity to share my life and my experience here with Donna and Robert Holt, JoJo Atkins, Stanley and Antoinette Ratliff, E. J., Tom and Carrie Moore, Anthony and B. J. Franklin, Carey and Melanie Casey, Mary Rhodes, Richard and Stephanie Townsell, William and Vanessa Little, Randy Brown, Precious Thomas, Willette Grant, Thomas and Tracie Worthy, Pat Herrod, Andy and Debbie Krumsieg, Lance and Cindy Greene, Drewone Goldsmith, Perry Bigelow, Dale and Reecie Craft, Geraldine Moore, Reba Charles, Belle Whaley, Art and Linda Jones, Stacey Smith, Mike and Karen Trout, Edward and Tanesha Daniels, Janice and Bill Rossbach, Phil and Kim Jackson, Jenai and Bryan Jenkins, Noel and Marianne Castellanos, Wanda Helm, Judy Kirkland, Dave and Tami Doig, Anthony and Marla Pegues, Roger and Tosha Love, Andrew and Daphne Moore, Walter Moore, Leo and Marie Barbie, Arthur Turner, Bernard and Brenda Harris, and many, many more. I love living in Lawndale.

BIBLIOGRAPHY

Bakke, Raymond. *The Urban Christian*. Downers Grove, Ill.: InterVarsity Press, 1987.

Claerbaut, David. *Urban Ministry*. Grand Rapids: Zondervan, 1984.

Friedman, Samuel. *Upon This Rock*. New York: Scribners, 1993.

Hacker, Andrew. *Two Nations: Black and White, Separate, Hostile, Unequal*. New York: Ballantine, 1992.

Kehrein, Glen, and Washington, Raleigh. *Breaking Down Walls*. Chicago: Moody, 1993.

Kotlowith, Alex. *There Are No Children Here*. New York: Doubleday, 1991.

Kunjufu, Jawanza. *Countering the Conspiracy to Destroy Black Boys*. Chicago: African American Images, 1985.

_____. *Countering the Conspiracy to Destroy Black Boys, Vol. II*. Chicago: African American Images, 1986.

_____. *Developing Positive Self-Images and Discipline in Black Children*. Chicago: African American Images, 1984.

_____. *Motivating and Preparing Black Youth to Work*. Chicago: African American Images, 1986.

Lemann, Nicholas. *The Promised Land*. New York: Alfred A. Knopf, 1991.

Lupton, Robert. *Theirs is the Kingdom*. San Francisco: Harper & Row, 1989.

Malcolm X. *The Autobiography of Malcolm X*. New York: Ballantine, 1973.

Nouwen, Henri. *In the Name of Jesus: Reflection on Christian Leadership*. New York: Crossroad, 1991.

Pannell, William. *The Coming Race Wars? A Cry for Reconciliation.* Grand Rapids: Zondervan, 1992.

Perkins, John. *Let Justice Roll Down.* Glendale, Calif.: Regal, 1976.

_____. *With Justice for All.* Ventura: Regal, 1982.

_____. *Beyond Charity: The Call to Christian Community Development.* Grand Rapids: Baker, 1993.

Perkins, Spencer, and Rice, Chris. *More than Equals: Racial Healing for the Sake of the Gospel.* Downers Grove: InterVarsity, 1993.

Weary, Dolphus. *I Ain't Comin' Back.* Wheaton: Tyndale, 1990.

West, Cornell. *Race Matters.* New York: Oxford University Press, 1993.

RESOURCES

1. The LCC Mission. The mission of the Lawndale Community Church is to redeem the "Lawndale Community." We seek to being Christian wholistic revitalization to the lives and environment of its residents through economic empowerment, housing improvement, educational enrichment, quality affordable health care, and Christian discipleship.

For further information, write or call:

Lawndale Community Church
3827 W. Ogden Ave.
Chicago, IL 60623
Phone: (312) 762–6389
Fax: (312) 762–5772

2. The CCDA Mission. The mission of the Christian Community Development Association is to develop a strong fellowship of those involved in Christian community development. CCDA desires to support and encourage existing Christian community developers and their ministries and help establish new Christian community development efforts.

For further information, write or call:

Christian Community Development Association
3827 W. Ogden Ave.
Chicago, IL 60623
Phone: (312) 762-0994
Fax: (312) 762-5772

3. *Urban Family* Magazine. For further information about *Urban Family* magazine, contact or call:

Urban Family Magazine
P.O. Box 32
Jackson, MS 39205–9930
Phone: (601) 354–1563
Fax: (601) 352–6882

"I LOVE LIVING IN LAWNDALE"

Printed in the United States
5834